Anne Cluysenaar

Introduction to Literary Stylistics

A discussion of dominant structures
in verse and prose

B. T. Batsford Limited
London

First published 1976
© Anne Cluysenaar, 1976
Cased edition ISBN 0 7134 2889 9
Limp edition ISBN 0 7134 2890 2

Printed by Bristol Typesetting Co Ltd
Barton Manor, St Philips, Bristol
for the publishers
B. T. Batsford Ltd
4 Fitzhardinge Street, London W1H 0AH

Contents

Acknowledgments

The Author and Publishers wish to thank the following for permission to reproduce the quotations appearing in this book (page references are to *Introduction to Literary Stylistics*):

C. Day Lewis, *Collected Poems*, Jonathan Cape/Hogarth Press (p. 45).

William Empson, *Seven Types of Ambiguity*, Chatto and Windus (pp. 50–51).

Brewster Ghiselin, *The Creative Poems*, Fontana (pp. 23–4, 38–9).

Robert Graves, *Selected Poems*, Penguin, and A. P. Watt (pp. 33, 57, 59).

Zbigniew Herbert, *Selected Poems*, Penguin, translated by Czislaw Milosz and Peter Dale-Scott (pp. 28–9).

D. H. Lawrence, *The Complete Poems*, Heinemann and 'The Blind Man' by courtesy of Laurence Pollinger Ltd and the Estate of the late Mrs Frieda Lawrence (pp. 63, 112–129).

F. R. Leavis, *Revaluation*, Chatto and Windus (p. 54).

Malcolm Lawry, *Under the Volcano*, Penguin (pp. 88, 89).

Wallace Stevens, *The Blue Guitar*, Faber & Faber (pp. 29–30, 30–1).

Summary of Chapters

Introduction
This book treats stylistics as an extension of practical criticism; texts as *acts of communication*, to which all features of language may contribute. Terminology is kept to a minimum although texts are explored in some analytic detail.

Linguistic criteria alone will not enable us to select the most relevant aspects of individual texts viewed as perceptual phenomena conveying unique meanings of intersubjective validity. The linguist and the literary critic both stand to gain from a study of how language works in *parole*. The relevance of perceptual psychology. Evaluation.

Chapter 1: Language, ' Reality', the Individual
Intersubjective validity of textual description. It's importance for teaching, criticism and the heightening of our perception.

Language. The medium of verbal art. Conventional and arbitrary. Creative of habits of perception which it can also be used to disturb.

' Reality'. Why language may seem to renew our perception of it. Norms. How linguistic and other norms may effect our perception of literary works. Unique interaction of elements in every text.

The Individual. Faced by ever-changing experience, he may attempt to give it expression through linguistic novelty. How the writer views language.

Chapter 2: Translation
Translation as an illustration of points made so far. A proper stylistic approach is vital to good translation: the text must be treated as a unique whole, never atomistically. Valéry's *Les Pas* translated by C. Day Lewis.

Chapter 3: Poetry

Practical implications of close attention to the linguistic aspects of utterances. Waley's *Swiftly the years* : comments by William Empson and Donald Davie. F. R. Leavis on Milton's *The hasty multitude*. . . .

Backgrounds of perception: Robert Graves' *Flying Crooked* illustrates some of the conflicting norms that may be relevant to a single text. Jan Mukařovsky's views inadequate to account for either perception or evalution. Longer textual studies: D. H. Lawrence's *Gloire de Dijon*, *The Falcon* or *Corpus Christi Carol*, Tennyson's *Now sleeps the crimson petal*. Dominance of some features over others in particular texts.

Chapter 4: Prose

Passages from Conrad, Dickens, Virginia Woolf, Lowry, Faulkner.

D. H. Lawrence's short story *The Blind Man* : dual structural/ semantic perspectives.

Chapter 5: Extensions and Summary

Summary of some aspects of foregoing discussions. Other ways of using stylistics, for example in the study of variant readings (W. B. Yeats' *Song of Wandering Aengus*), ' register ' (H. Reed's *Judging Distances*), literary echoes (Keats' *Ode to a Nightingale* and Shakespeare's *To be or not to be*).

Some rules of thumb for textual analysis, but flexibility (avoidance of preconceptions as to what features are likely to be important in a given text) essential. Evaluation again.

Preface

This book has been written in response to certain questions repeatedly posed by those who doubt the relevance of linguistics to literary studies and, more generally, the value of analytical knowledge in an area of profound emotional involvement. The questions I have most often been asked, over the past ten years, have also been my own most immediate ones. Can stylistics help to make more conscious, and more describable, delicate interactions of form and meaning which appear to elude even close criticism? Is there any sense in which such consciousness is bound to destroy literature : our reactions to it, or the writer's creative impulse (since, after all, many writers now go through higher education)? As a writer myself and teacher of creative writing (as well as critic of contemporary poetry), this second question, in all its ramifications, seems to me of great importance. I have come to feel that the answer to both depends on how we *use* linguistic theory and information. The emphasis of this book falls on the attempt to see linguistic features never in isolation but always in relation to each other and to the whole work (or passage) in which they occur, the work itself being seen as a unified communicative event. When this is done, I believe that the answer to the first question is ' yes ', and that the insight thus gained into verbal creativity results in an emphatic ' no ' to the second. Stylistic exploration can be the equivalent, for literature, of the painter's or sculptor's workshop, and can acquaint the student far more intimately than is otherwise possible with the working preoccupation of writers with the restrictions and possibilities of the verbal medium.

In order to be adequate to the purpose, the discussion that follows has had to be presented in as untechnical a way as possible and yet to reach well below the surface of the subject.

The research worker already committed to stylistics will therefore find that the book has many very obvious limitations. I have avoided flashing what linguistic teeth I may have acquired from linguistics, while at the same time attempting to involve the reader at some imaginative and analytical depth in the exploration of linguistic events. I have avoided the tedium, and jettisoned the rigour, of pointing out every junction at which critical statements 'switch from (various levels of) description to evaluation, nor have I always overtly ' retrieved ' my critical remarks by showing how they can be related to the linguistic evidence. The price seemed worth paying – for a readable text, and especially perhaps for readers interested enough to go on from it to make these distinctions for themselves : finding on the whole, I hope, that my remarks are not inextricably ' mixed ' (in the first sphere) nor without satisfactory textual foundation (in the second).

It seemed sensible, for similar reasons, to restrict reference, as far as compatible with a proper coverage of the issues, to a group of books easily to be found. I have therefore referred frequently to various anthologies which contain papers in stylistics drawn from various, more scattered, sources. Again, wishing to keep the main text uncluttered, I have made the notes rather more substantial than may be customary : the reader is therefore particularly encouraged to consult them after, if not during, his or her reading of each chapter.

Procedures of analysis are not discussed except in outline. Every critic will find his own way of working, while teachers of stylistics who find this book useful will be far better able than I am (by their knowledge of the student and of the work to be done) to suggest productive approaches. Research workers may find that the studies undertaken here, because of rather than despite the ' bird's eye view ' adopted, offer an interesting contrast to the close and necessarily limited analysis which often has to form the backbone of a thesis.

Stylistics is presented here as an extension of practical criticism, enabling the critic to sensitise his grasp of detail *together with* his grasp of structured wholes. I have also had in the forefront of my mind the need to provide a basis for teaching which is more open to question by the student than is traditional practical criticism, while also forming a firm foundation for undergraduate research. I have, in fact, to thank many of my former and present students for the keenness with which they have explored, whether angrily or delightedly, the difficulties and insights offered by the adaptation of linguistics to literary purposes. Writing this book has been a pleasure because it is the outcome of so many friendly discussions.

Of course linguistics bears on literary studies in many ways which are not my subject here. The rather cumbersome title is intended to indicate the book's limitations in this respect. I should also like it to suggest that stylistics itself be regarded as a widening, not as a narrowing, of critical range, a tool to be used when the general critical context requires, in conjunction with other 'intrinsic' methods of study, and with 'extrinsic' approaches involving other disciplines such as psychology, history, politics, sociology. Indeed, since the stylistic approach adopted insists on the contextualisation of linguistic features within the total microcosm of the work, it leads naturally on to the further contextualisation of the work itself in the social macrocosm. At that point, psycho and socio linguistics have a great deal to offer the critic, though they lie beyond the scope of this book.

I wish particularly to thank those students who have at various times read versions and parts of this book and made detailed and helpful comments. I have also to thank Professor William Haas, of Manchester, Professor John Sinclair, now my colleague at Birmingham, and Dr Geoffrey Leech, of Lancaster, for having over several years discussed stylistics with me and read the manuscript in various stages of unreadiness. I am very much aware of how much I owe to these and other friends, both academically and personally, and of how little this book can satisfy them or me, except perhaps as a preliminary exploration into areas we all, well beyond the duty of professional involvement, find so enjoyable.

For Walt

For I still think of life as once of mist in Cornwall
Man-high and from the sea subsiding gently
Over the ploughed fields, brown, with scarce green growth,
But hidden under field-grey all that day,
Woven to one opacity.
Then on my eyesight the slant light broke
Of a single mist-drop narrowly slung to a cobweb
And each, the mist, through which my senses travelled
Broke at that sun-reflecting signal to its own:
The watered air grew bright with single claws:
So on the fine web spun from something stronger
One man can hold, precarious, complete
His own life's light that never is repeated
But acts as orrery to all the lights of others:
And that same web grows finer with its function,
More beautiful to praise with each drop held
In that peculiar tension once forever.

James Burns Singer,
From Corner Boy's Farewell

Introduction

There are many ways in which the theories, techniques and descriptions of modern linguistics are being, and might be, used in the study of literature.[1] I have concerned myself in this book with just one possibility, partly because it seems to have been relatively neglected and raises questions of importance for stylistics as a whole, and partly because it follows naturally from the more valid orientations of practical criticism.[2] My aim has been to use linguistics as a means of studying individual texts as wholes rather than of tabulating, for example, the stylistic traits of a work, writer or period.[3] Each text, whether a whole work or a passage, is treated here as an act of communication to which all features of language, including meaning, contribute.[4] I hope that the reader, particularly the reader encountering stylistics for the first time, will find that this way of working comes easily and allows him or her to pursue in detail, and with sensitivity, what is after all the primary aim of literary criticism, the exploration of meanings conveyed by language.

Accordingly, although the practical studies include some fairly close description, I have kept the linguistic analysis[5] as uncomplicated as possible and terminology to a minimum. The linguistically trained reader will find that he could go much further into detail and also formalise his results to a higher degree.[6] For him, the interest of these studies will lie in the questions they raise, questions which are scarcely being asked and which are crucial. The fact that they cannot yet be answered should not lead stylistics to busy itself with other things but, on the contrary, to define and investigate them. We must accept already, I think, that certain techniques of linguistic description are, when applied to literature, inappropriate or incomplete (as literary critics have been pointing out for some time)[7] and this negative clarification would be of great use if it helped stylistics to develop in more difficult, but more relevant, directions.[8]

My own basic assumption has been that the mere linguistic description of a text is just applied linguistics, not 'stylistics'. All description is selective. If it were not, the critic would simply have to hand over the entire text. And the problem of selection has been the (not always recognised) bone of contention in recent controversies over the relevance of linguistics to literary criticism. I take the view that, if we want to pick out from amongst the mass of linguistic features in any text those that are of *special* importance to the reader – the receiver of communication – our criteria of selection cannot remain solely linguistic.[9] Many linguistic features will be doing no more than their everyday communicative job : they could not be omitted from the text, but they play no special role in it. The stylistician will, as a result, want to omit from his description many features properly described by the linguist and will mention others to which the linguist, *as* linguist, cannot justify giving special (or perhaps any) attention.[10] What this may mean in practice will become evident in the practical studies that follow. The main point now is that linguistic description offers the stylistician (or literary critic) both too much and too little.[11] And this is why critics have sometimes accused stylistics of irrelevance to literary concerns. One must admit that it has taken stylisticians with a primarily linguistic training some time to see the force of these accusations, which have not always been put very clearly.[12] Of late, however, stylistics itself has faced the same problem in a different guise. It has become evident that two stylisticians, even working with the same linguistic model, do not necessarily arrive at the same description of a given text.[13] Is this a matter of individual predisposition? Or of partial descriptions that might be fused into a higher unity? What is certain is that in such cases we *already have* non-linguistic selection (I am leaving aside mere differences of presentation). And it seems likely that the different descriptions that may result are mainly due to the lack of a coherent framework *other than the linguistic* to guide the process of selection[14] – a framework, in other words, of stylistic theory, or theories, to which any description might be explicitly referred. As will become obvious in the practical work, the resulting descriptions might often be of ambiguous structures (analogous to the visual ambiguities so interesting to *gestalt* psychology).[15] No doubt such structures are responsible for many apparent 'disagreements' in description, and in that case what we could hope for would be a better-articulated relationship between two or more acceptable views. This book does not attempt to lay the groundwork for a theory of stylistics; but it demonstrates, I hope, some of the factors that should be taken into account by anyone with that aim in mind.

It may already be suspected that stylistics, on my showing, has a great deal to learn from perceptual psychology present and to come.[16] The research that will show how we perceive auditory structures in time, when these are multi-level processes like acts of speech, has yet to be carried out. But to state that a literary work is a perceptual object taking time to unfold before the reader[17] is to state the obvious, though little enough attention is paid even to the obvious implications (implications, for example, for the interpretation of the *effects* of rhyme).[18] A part or aspect is perceived in relation to other parts or aspects, and in relation to the whole, bearing time in mind, and the same linguistic feature may therefore appear 'different' in different (simultaneous or sequential) contexts.[19] Again, different linguistic features, if they function in the same way, may strike the reader as similar. The stylistician must not behave like a rigid geometrician, insisting that the two horizontal lines on the right in Figure 1 are equal in length, just like the two on the left.

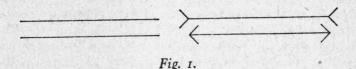

Fig. 1.

Of course, they are. But in their changed context, they seem different, the one below appearing shorter than the other. No critic of painting who ignored this perceptual effect would be considered reliable, however geometrically accurate his observations might be.[20] This is a very simple illustration, even where visual matters are concerned. Meaning does not apparently enter here, while in other semi-representational figures it has been shown to influence perception;[21] and indeed the famous Rorschach blot test shows that completely external semantic factors also affect it (the test would otherwise be useless in psychiatry as an aid to the diagnosis of individual preoccupations). The problems raised, then, are considerable. But ignoring them will not make them go away.

The truly accurate description of any perceptual object is not that which, to use the visual analogy again, stops at the geometrical qualities of the lines – and which therefore 'destroys' other qualities that appear to belong to them in context – but one which captures their perceptual inequality.[22] This can be no excuse, though, for not *knowing* that the lines are geometrically equal. Not to know this obscures, in fact, a most interesting problem, even in such a simple case as that illustrated in Figure 1. What of the far more complex problems (mysteries) that must be lying unexplored in works of verbal art? Those who have objected to close linguistic description *per se* are not speaking in the name of enlightenment but of obscurantism. The genuine issue is that of relevance, not of detail, and neither quality must be sacrificed. It even seems that linguistics as well as literary criticism has something interesting to learn from a stylistics able to satisfy both requirements, since linguistics will hardly have discovered 'how language works' until it knows more of how it works in individual utterances, in *parole*.[23] Of the type of stylistics I have in mind, the term 'exploration' seems more appropriate than 'analysis' and it is therefore the former term that I shall generally prefer, just as I shall prefer 'reader' to 'critic' when I wish to focus on the perceptual rather than evaluative role.

Evaluation is, however, part of the critic's job, and since it is an important part, it should follow only after every effort has been made to see the work from all relevant points of view, extrinsic as well as intrinsic.[24] We evaluate after all, for many different purposes, and the literary critic must be free to give the fullest possible account of his subject. I shall return to this question towards the end of the book.[25] Meanwhile, however, it seems necessary to point out that, whatever other forms of evaluation may ultimately be relevant to a cultural object, one which remains central to literary criticism, as against any other kind of criticism, is that which concerns itself with the particular *medium*, language, as it is deployed in the act of communication. This is what distinguishes literary evaluation from any other kind: other forms of judgement apply equally, *mutatis mutandis*, to other arts and objects. And it is to this uniquely literary evaluation that stylistics can bring not only descriptive tools but eventually, I believe, important concepts drawn from both linguistics and perceptual psychology.[26]

Chapter I

Before committing oneself to a detailed study of language, it is only intelligent to ask whether language is worth so much attention. Could we not 'go straight to meaning' and discuss that? After all, I have myself admitted in the introduction that I consider meaning the ultimate goal of critical exploration. But the more the reader already knows about language, and especially if he has tried to write creatively,[1] the less it will fall to me to convince him of the fact that the full meaning of any text arises from intricacies of formal and semantic interaction.[2] No act of communication, much less the subtle uses of language we tend to call ' literature ', can be treated dualistically, as if ' form ' and ' meaning ' were not merely separately *describable* (up to a point) but actually separable.[3] The significance (if we restrict the meaning of 'meaning' for a moment) of any linguistic event arises from its entire structure. And who would want to discuss anything less than that kind of full meaning? Indeed, that is what 'meaning', in the literary sense, has always meant. Stylistics here enters into the mainstream of modern critical thought.

Those of us who expect to talk or write a good deal about literature are, of course, in a special position. However accurate our intuitions may be, unless we can show how they arise from the text, we shall be merely exhorting, even browbeating, our audience. And if, moreover, our responses do not have inter-subjective validity, we shall be writing autobiography rather than criticism. Responses that are totally subjective (as well as unexplained), though they may properly play a large part in our private approaches to literature, can have no part in public discussion, simply because they are irrelevant to the responses of others. Unless, of course, their response is not to the text at all but to ourselves – to the ' journey of a soul amongst master-pieces'. In order to clarify what is subjective and what is *inter*-subjective, we need to know a great deal about how language and perception work. And in order to be able to describe the features of the text from which our responses arise with an accuracy adequate to their subtle nature, we need the best modes of description available. Even the most sensitive intuitions may be distorted if inadequate tools are used to explicate them.[4] Where what we have to describe are linguistic features, there can be no rival to contemporary linguistics as a source of such descriptions. In this respect, modern literary criticism has still to realise that previous critical periods were less fortunate.

But those who do not expect to talk professionally or other-wise about their responses to literature will find that there are also more private reasons for understanding language. As speakers of English, we might think that conscious understanding is unnecessary. And, in principle, perhaps it is. But human responses are generally developed to less than their full capacity : I have found in practice that I tend to notice what I can describe, and many people I have worked with have told me the same thing, finding (sometimes with surprise) that their responses to the text deepened as they deepened their understanding of its language. Goethe, who should have known, made a similar observation to a young man who asked him for advice, being doubtful of the value of analysis. ' Do not be afraid,' Goethe told him, ' of taking a poem to pieces.[5] I know of no other way to pass from a general to a particular appreciation.' The same applies, of course, to prose.[6] No doubt Goethe was so well aware of this because, as a writer, he had discovered that conscious linguistic knowledge, knowledge of the medium, is necessary to support even the most powerful inspiration – perhaps it is *most* necessary to it, since powerful emotional or intellectual passions tend to disrupt our powers of communication, especially if we are exploring new areas of human experience. If readers are to be capable of responding to language as writers would wish, they must eventually make the same discovery as the writers themselves.[7] As Winifred Nowottny puts it, ' we must, when reading as critics, allow due importance to each and all of the levels at which poetry elaborates its effects, if the reputa-tions of the poets are to be safe in our hands'.[8] But this is true of any reading whatever. Our capacities for response, no matter how fine, may always be made still more sensitive by that effort of attention which arises naturally from a desire to savour to the full the nature of what moves us. It has often struck me that an impressionistic critic's approach to literature shares something of the Petrarchan lover's approach to his mistress: he does not wish to know her fully because he suspects that her magical charm will vanish. His sense of her true mystery is too superficial to withstand the impact of reality. Anyone who has caught a genuine glimpse of the importance of language in human life, however, need never fear that he can dissipate its wonder with what William Empson once called, in a not dissimilar context, 'a little scratching'.[9]

The rest of this chapter is concerned with discussing, mainly with the non-linguistic reader, certain important aspects of language which may not be obvious to him: especially, its status as a 'system of signs', its relationship to 'reality', and the restrictions and opportunities with which it confronts individual expression and creativity. We shall be looking a good deal, for reasons that must already be clear, at what creative writers have had to say about verbal art and the processes of composition.[10] In Chapter II, we shall consider the special case of literary translation, in order to show how a writer's effects and meanings may be dependent upon the medium in which they are first elaborated. The better the writer, as a verbal artist, the harder he or she will be to translate adequately since, added to the normal inseparability of form and meaning, there will be the stylistic exploitation of accidental features peculiar to the original language-system.[11]

First, then, what *is* a 'language-system'? The reader who wants any kind of detailed answer will need to go to the linguistic literature. Here, however, we can at least consider a few aspects that are of particular intrinsic interest and also of importance for stylistics.

Modern linguistics has shown that natural languages are not ragbag aggregates of elements, but *systems* in which all elements are ultimately interrelated. At any one period of time, a speaker has at his disposal a fixed number of sounds, words and ways in which these may be combined ('phonotactic' and 'syntactic' regularities). These the linguist describes in the phonology, vocabulary and grammar of each language. Almost all the elements of any language either *have* or *distinguish* meanings.[12] For example, the words 'doe' and 'go' both have meanings;

the sounds /d/ and /g/ distinguish these meanings (since the rest of the words is the same, /-əʊ/).[13] However, this difference of sound remains unnoticed by most speakers of English in contexts where it cannot distinguish meanings, for example in the context /-ləʊ /: whichever of the two sounds /d/ or /g/ I pronounce before /l/, the listener will normally 'hear' the word he would spell as *glow*. The same applies to /t/ and /k/ before /l/ word-initially, as the reader can test for himself in a word such as 'clean'. This phenomenon is a regular feature of English phonology, a convention, not a coincidence. We are not free to invent words beginning with /dl/ or /tl/ to be distinguished by this alone from words beginning with /gl/ or /kl/. Consequently, we find it hard to notice such distinctions in other languages. Our own linguistic habits interfere and restructure the objective acoustic facts. This is a clear illustration, in one small detail, of the conventional nature of natural language.

Further, the signs of which languages are made up are arbitrary, in that there is no reason why a given aspect of inner or outer 'reality' should be 'meant' by a particular syntactical structure or sound. In English, the sounds meaning 'sun' and 'son' happen to be the same.[14] In French, they are different. A pun is possible in English that is not possible in French. On the other hand, the word for 'sun' in French rhymes with the word for 'bee' and with that for 'sleep', which has proved convenient in innumerable love-poems. The point is, of course, that the writer's formal and semantic material is different depending on the language. He generally attempts to 'redeem' the 'accidents' of his particular linguistic code[15] by assigning to them aesthetic or communicative roles, or both, aided by the common human tendency to see forms as significant.[16] The result is what W. K. Wimsatt referred to as 'iconic' language.[17] And it is this which makes literary translation even more difficult than non-literary, since no two languages offer the same range of 'accidents'.[18] But we shall return to translation in Chapter II. Meanwhile, we must bear in mind the conventional and arbitrary nature of the verbal medium. A language (or *langue*) is primarily a relational structure. It can manifest itself in different material forms, other than those which happen to make up its actual phonology. It may manifest itself instead in writing or in the auditory (or written) 'dots and dashes' of the morse code. It could also manifest itself in a different set of spoken sounds. Provided the code allows for the same distinctions, and is under-

stood and received, ordinary communication remains undis-
turbed, just as a game of chess can be played if we replace the
conventional figures with any other objects that allow the same
permutations.

With the relatively fixed elements and patterns of his language,
which bear no direct relationship to 'reality', man attempts to
handle and express ever-changing aspects of experience.[19] The
possible combinations are fortunately infinite, as Henry Miller
remarks in one of the autobiographical passages below. In fact,
most sentences, however ordinary they may seem, are unique.
That type of uniqueness, though, is not enough for many writers.
They tend to search for a 'voice' of their own, a way of using
language that is peculiar to themselves, even perhaps in some
ways abnormal.[20] But of course, however far they go in this
direction, they must somehow still communicate, and they can
only do so by preserving enough of a relationship with the
accepted code for the reader to decode a message. Every utterance, however deviant, is understood, if at all, only against the
background of a language-system, or systems (in the case, for
example, of multilingual puns), of intersubjective validity. There
is no such thing as a completely subjective or 'private' language.
This, then, is how Miller describes the experience of finding his
own voice: not a private language, but a way of recombining
and perhaps partially distorting pre-existent elements.

I began by examining the style and technique of those whom
I once admired and worshipped: Nietzsche, Dostoievski,
Hamsun, even Thomas Mann, who today I discard as being
a skilful fabricator, a brickmaker, an inspired jackass or
draught-horse. I imitated every style in the hope of finding
the clue to the gnawing secret of how to write. Finally I came
to a dead end, to a despair and desperation few men have
known, because there was no divorce between myself as writer
and myself as man: to fail as a writer meant to fail as a man.
And I failed. I realised that I was nothing – less than nothing – a minus quantity. It was at this point, in the dead
Sargasso Sea, so to speak, that I really began to write. I
began from scratch, throwing everything overboard, even
those I most loved. Immediately I heard my own voice I was
enchanted: the fact that it was a separate, distinct, unique
voice sustained me. . . . I had to grow foul with knowledge,
realise the futility of everything, smash everything, grow

desperate, then humble, then sponge myself off the slate, as it were, in order to recover my authenticity. I had to arrive at the brink and then take a leap in the dark.[21]

I talk now about Reality, but I know there is no way of getting at it, leastways by writing.[22]

And again, Miller has discovered that, in language,

One can only go forward by going backward and then sideways and then up and then down. There is no progress: there is perpetual movement, displacement, which is circular, spiral, endless.[23]

This description of linguistic creation is all the more convincing for being given in apparent opposition to professional students of language.

I do not believe in words, no matter if strung together by the most skilful man: I believe in language, which is something beyond words, something which words give only an inadequate illusion of. Words do not exist separately, except in the minds of scholars, etymologists, philologists, etc. Words divorced from language are dead things, and yield no secrets. A man is revealed in his style, the language he has created for himself.

By 'language', Miller clearly means something very close to what the modern linguist means, though at the time the passages were written it would have been difficult for him to be aware of this. Miller's introduction of the notion of reality – the implication that he is in search of it and yet knows that ' there is no way of getting at it, leastways by writing ' – brings us round, similarly, to the linguist's view of the relationship, in Benjamin Lee Whorf's words, of ' language, thought and reality'. Whorf believed that ' we dissect reality along lines laid down by our native languages '.

Every language is a vast pattern-system, different from others, in which are culturally ordained the forms and categories by which the personality not only communicates, but also analyses nature, notices or neglects types of relationship and phenomena, channels his reasoning, and builds the house of his consciousness.[24]

More recently, taking into account developments in philosophy since Whorf's time, William Haas put the matter very clearly.

> It is of course, ultimately, some relation of linguistic expressions to other things that constitutes their meanings. The question is : What sort of relation? My point is that it is not, and cannot be, a relation between two distinct orders of thing. The alleged confrontation of language with facts, the alleged reference of expressions to things uninvolved in language – this we cannot make sense of. If we divide language from other things in this dualist fashion, both are dissolved in a general blur. It is only in their active interplay with one another that either assumes determinate shape; and it is this *interplay* – this active co-operation of utterances with things – that constitutes the meanings of utterances.[25]

Or, to put it in Joseph Conrad's succinct phrase, ' things " as they are " exist in words '.[26] That is why the words, or rather language, are so important. They are an opportunity as well as an evidently arbitrary limitation, affecting differently individuals born into different language-groups. That is also why the individual's knowledge of, and selection from, his language is so vital a matter. His perceptual and inner world is, it seems, largely articulated even to himself within the confines of his linguistic awareness, and is certainly expressed to the reader solely through the forms he has chosen from amongst those available to him.[27] The ' streams of energy playing upon us '[28] may remain unknown in themselves, being filtered to us through what Ted Hughes has called ' doubtful and provisional senses '.[29] Like the senses, however, language offers opportunities for the articulation of life. Without it, as Helen Keller's autobiographical writings convince us, we lack an important means of elaborating our contacts with others and even with ourselves. This, too, is the point of William Golding's use of a restricted language for Neanderthal man in his novel *The Inheritors*,[30] and of the special language with which Faulkner endows the sensitive but underdeveloped Benjy in *The Sound and the Fury*.[31] Not only in such cases, but in all uses of language, a world-view is being, more or less consistently and fully, elaborated. Shakespeare's extraordinary linguistic range, Gerard Manley Hopkins's more restricted but distinctive and consistent idiolect, serve ultimately the same purpose : the exploration of individual consciousness and of the reality to which it is a living, if partial, witness. The result is that when we read a writer who has found his voice, however wide-ranging or limited that voice may be, it seems as if, in Wallace Stevens's lines,

> It was everything being more real, himself
> At the centre of reality, seeing it.
> It was everything bulging and blazing and big in itself.[32]

Not that we have come any nearer to the ' bare facts ', but we seem to see life in a new way because of the properties of the mediating language, its relationship to the modes of language with which we are already familiar – and therefore also to our previous experience of realities.[33] Reading at this level of awareness does not present us with an escapist (substitute) reality. It involves us in contact with the very edges of our previous being. Moreover, as linguists have pointed out, language is of more than immediate personal, or indeed public, importance to man, since it is the vehicle of ' non-biological heredity ', the vehicle (that is) of our contacts with the past and the future as well as the present.

What follows is a discussion of the three basic points of reference for verbal creativity: reality, language and the individual's relation to both. Although in focusing on any one of these we are inevitably dealing with all three, let us take them up one after the other here so as to circumscribe areas of special relevance for stylistics. The reader will bear with me, I hope, where I find it necessary to refer to ideas already mentioned, in order to relate them now to more detailed contexts.

Reality

I have said that, as we conceive of our position in the universe nowadays, ' reality ' no longer seems to us the simple object upon which Dr Johnson stubbed his toe. We still stub our toes, of course – we split the atom – but we no longer think that we know just what we are in contact with when we do.

This predominantly modern view is not that which presented itself to most of our predecessors. Since they tended to assume that what they saw all around them *was* reality, they also tended to feel that language acted as some sort of ' veil ' coming between them and things as they really are – or else, as in Shelley's words, they saw poetry as the great revealer: 'a poem is the very image of life expressed in its eternal truth ', reaching beyond appearances. Such is the idea, perhaps, that lies behind Jean Cocteau's description of poetry's action on the senses.

> Suddenly, as if in a flash, we *see* the dog, the coach, the house for the first time. Shortly afterwards habit erases again this potent image. We pet the dog, we call the coach, we live in the house; we do not see them any more. Such is the role of poetry. It takes off the veil, in the full sense of the word.[34]

Both these views of reality – that it is hidden, or that it is revealed, by language – make the assumption, as I have already suggested, that reality is not only independent of our perception of it (a perception at least partly conditioned by language) but also independently *observable*, so that we can, as it were, check the degree of accuracy with which language relates to it, 'match our pictures with the real thing '. But such an idea meets insurmountable difficulties and modern philosophy has on the whole accepted that reality is not observable in some neutral way, without the distortions of a medium, whether the medium be that of natural or of scientific language (leaving aside the basic medium of the human senses). This was Haas's point. Or as Shelley said, 'all things exist as they are perceived: at least in relation to the percipient '.[35] He went on to make a suggestion that relates closely to modern notions of linguistic creativity, claiming that poetry replenishes the imagination with thoughts which 'form new intervals and interstices whose void forever craves fresh food ' – in other words, the habits of perception to which Cocteau refers are disturbed by the way in which poetic (I would simply say, all creative) language works. Just as, when the senses are awakened by drugs or by any other experience, we may seem to see a new world – so, if the habits of language are disturbed, the world *we see* does actually alter, no matter whether the result is a world more 'real' than that which we saw before: even the question is often meaningless, since there is seldom any conceivable way of answering it.[36]

It seems clear, then, that although language will not get at 'things in themselves ', as Miller knew, it serves us in our attempt to make contact with 'what there is '. In Wallace Stevens's words, 'it is not only that the imagination adheres to reality, but, also, that reality adheres to the imagination and that the interdependence is essential '.[37] The words of poet and linguist are almost the same. The thought has been sweetly elaborated by the Polish poet Zbigniew Herbert.[38]

I would like to describe the simplest emotion
joy or sadness
but not as others do
reaching for shafts of rain or sun

I would like to describe a light
which is being born in me
but I know it does not resemble
any star
for it is not so bright
not so pure
and is uncertain

I would like to describe courage
without dragging behind me a dusty lion
and also anxiety
without shaking a glass full of water

To put it another way
I would give all metaphors
in return for one word
drawn out of my breast like a rib
for one word
contained within the boundaries
of my skin

but apparently this is not possible

and just to say – I love
I run round like mad
picking up handfuls of birds
and my tenderness
which after all is not made of water
asks the water for a face

and anger
different from fire
borrows from it
a loquacious tongue

So is blurred
so is blurred
in me
what white-haired gentlemen
separated once and for all
and said
this is the subject
and this is the object

We fall asleep
with one hand under our head
and with the other in a mound of planets

our feet abandon us
and taste the earth
with their tiny roots
which each morning
we tear up painfully

Language

All language is in a fundamental sense creative, as we have
seen, but the kind of creativity Shelley, Cocteau, Stevens and
Herbert are describing is a creativity to which both the writer
and the reader are sensitive, not the 'creation' of a world of
regular habits which tend to drop below the threshold of consciousness. The creativity of ordinary language *can* be felt, however, when we move from one language to another, or even
from one dialect to another within the one language. New
locutions often seem fresher, even more accurate, than familiar
phrases.[39] Unfamiliar uses[40] of our own language-dialect strike
us in the same way and this is a large part of their value. Wallace
Stevens, preoccupied all his poetic life with these matters, has
expressed the unspoken demand of readers to writer in his poem
The Blue Guitar – the 'blue guitar' being, of course, language.

They said, 'You have a blue guitar.
You do not play things as they are.'

The man replied, 'Things as they are
Are changed upon the blue guitar.'

And they said then, 'But play, you must,
A tune beyond us yet ourselves,

> A tune upon the blue guitar
> Of things exactly as they are.' [41]

The writer must use – even where he departs from – the conventions of his language. Donald Davie pointed this out when he wrote : ' The freshness of perception which every good writer wants to attain, every good reader wants to recognise and respond to – this comes normally by way of convention, not in despite of it.'[42] (In the present context one might well drop ' normally '.) The apparent paradox may become clearer if we consider the visual arts, since there it is no more than self-evident that, as Gombrich says, the artist ' cannot transcribe what he sees; he can only translate it into the terms of his medium ', pencil, paint, clay.[43] Moreover, he continues, ' the style, like the medium, creates a mental set which makes the artist look for certain aspects in the scene around him which he can render. Painting is an activity, and the artist will therefore tend to see what he paints rather than to paint what he sees.'[44] Again, the reader, like the observer of a painting, ' decodes ' the message (and responds to the material aesthetically) in accordance with a background of previous artistic experience. In the case of texts, in fact, the distinct structures of *parole* exist only thanks to their relationship to *langue*. Without this, we should see only squiggles on paper, or hear only blurred vocal noises. Linguistic conventions are in themselves no barrier to creativity or its reception : they are their condition, they constitute the essential background out of which verbal art is made. ' The artist works within a structured area of problems ',[45] also, in the stylistic and cultural sense. No doubt classical art has always been more inclined to acknowledge this than romantic art, but it remains equally true of any art whatever. In romantic art, departure from expectations may be greater and more frequent, but the back-cloth against which it makes its impact and sense is – has to be – the very conventions that are being flouted. The use to which classical art puts the medium may tend to be ' abnormal ' in a different way : by the unusual degree of appropriateness to meaning, rather than by the deviance, of its structures.

It will be worth pausing here to consider in more detail some of the ways in which language may be unexpected and so renew our perception both of itself and of the world. The process is, essentially, that described by Roman Jakobson when he wrote that the aim of poetry is to point out that the word is not identical with its referent – that there is a gap between linguistic meanings and the non-linguistic phenomena to which they refer.[46]

> It was when I said,
> 'There is no such thing as the truth',
> That the grapes grew fatter.
> The fox ran out of his hole.[47]

Literature can deviate against the language-system itself, speech-expectations or, indeed, against expectations that have been set up in the work we are reading.[48] And these various kinds of deviation can involve departures from expectations regarding different 'levels' of language, semantic, lexical, grammatical, phonolog-ical, and different 'ranks' within grammar and phonology (at the rank of sentence or phrase, for example, within English grammar; or at the rank of phoneme, syllable or foot within English phon-ology).[49] Deviations may become perceptible when we look 'along' the text at any one rank or level, or they may strike us only when we correlate linguistic events at different ranks or levels, as when we notice for instance that every sentence begins with the same word or sound. Further, deviations may appear appropriate to the meaning (in a number of ways) or not. And finally, formal structures that are not *in themselves* unexpected in any way may still relate to meaning with an appropriateness which we do not expect to discover in ordinary, non-literary, language.[50]

These remarks could of course be greatly elaborated. We bring to our reception of a text the multiplicity of expectations that are built into living in this culture at this time as inheritors of a particular past. We may also attempt to reproduce in ourselves the expectations operating at previous periods, so as to approach an older text as nearly as possible in the way in which contempo-raries would have approached it. Consequently, even what is 'in' the text alters with time. The difficulty of determining just how norms, even linguistic norms, are established need not make it impossible for us to acknowledge their influence on perception, or to discuss the problems that arise in understanding how they function – when, for example, there appears to be a 'clash' of norms, a given structure being interpreted as 'normal' against one and 'abnormal' against the other. In my view, it would be unrealistic to solve such a problem by claiming that one type of norm (say, the literary) always wins over some other type (say, that of speech).[51] The best that can be said for such blanket solutions is that they save the critic a headache which he ought to have. They short-circuit proper inquiry. It seems more likely, on the evidence of practical experience, that each work sets up, by the way in which its particular elements interact, a balance of forces which must be understood as a unique structure.[52] When general principles emerge, one might expect them to have to do with complex formal pressures and counterpressures within such a structure, and to take into account the tendency to interpret the whole significantly.[53] This tendency may be illustrated in relation to the shape in Figure 2.

Fig. 2.

Our interpretation of the dot to the left can be influenced either from outside the figure, that is by labelling it as a duck or as a rabbit, or from inside, by adding to the picture features associated with either animal (whether with its own shape or its environment).[54] According to the pressure of significance, the dot will appear either negligible (at most an irrelevant blot on the back of the duck's head, or even a fault in the paper) or important (the rabbit's nose). The stylistician will not, I believe, be having it both ways if he must sometimes argue that a formal feature *present* in a work is more or less prominent according to its semantic *relevance*.[55] The plausibility of the argument will partly depend, however, on the intrinsic prominence of the feature itself :[56] if we increase the size of the dot, at a certain point we will be forced to admit that its prominence cannot be reduced by the context. We shall be forced to interpret it as a 'fault' in the drawing of a duck or to interpret the figure as a rabbit, whatever the label or the environment may suggest. The dot can no longer blend into the perceptual background.[57]

With these thoughts in mind, the reader may care to explore for himself this little poem by Robert Graves, in which initial syntactical (and other) distortion and disturbance give way to relative regularity, while the rhyme-scheme and metre remain neatly conventional throughout, reminiscent of the kind of moralising poem this certainly is not – or is it? The interaction of various norms in this poem is complex.

> The butterfly, the cabbage-white,
> (His honest idiocy of flight)
> Will never now, it is too late,
> Master the art of flying straight,
> Yet has – who knows so well as I? –
> A just sense of how not to fly:
> He lurches here and here by guess
> And God and hope and hopelessness.
> Even the aerobatic swift
> Has not his flying-crooked gift.[58]

Though change is constantly going on in language, so that the analogy of language-systems to chess is not in all respects accurate, we have seen that the individual has at his disposal at any one time a fixed number of elements and 'rules' for their combination into sentences. He can infringe these rules, add to them, or relate the structure of his language to meaning in ways that are not positively prescribed by everyday linguistic convention. But he cannot work right outside conventions. On the contrary, to succeed in linguistic communication he must use convention for his own purposes : it is an indispensable support to him in the search for originality of thought and expression.

The work of verbal art thus has a structure which is neither objective nor subjective, but intersubjective. The reader who wishes to discuss with others his reaction to a work relies on the fact that his reactions and theirs share certain features. And although some of his, and their, reactions are necessarily restricted or private (hence, of course, the value for individual psychology of word-association tests), these reactions do not form the basis for discussion, since however deeply they may affect the individual, they are not, intersubjectively, 'in' the work.[59] The reactions that *do* form the basis of discussion are those which the language-system and the culture in which it operates make (or, in the case of an older text, made) a common

c

ground of reference.[60] Sensitivity of reaction varies with individuals, with experience of reading, and with mood and situation. But a solid intersubjective basis remains. If I miss something, you can 'show' me that it is there. And that is one of the purposes of most useful literary discussion.

' Correction ' of one's own writing or of other people's (editorially, in creative writing courses, amongst friends) is a matter of making ourselves more fully aware of the potentialities of the medium.[61] The kind of thinking often involved in creative writing is described by Paul Valéry, with the obvious intention of startling the uninitiated.

> I am looking for a word (*says the poet*) a word which shall be :
> feminine,
> with two syllables,
> containing P or F,
> ending on a mute ' e ',
> and synonym of shattering, disintegration;
> and not learned, not rare.
> Six conditions – at least![62]

The reader may test his knowledge of French by finding the word Valéry was looking for. Of course, that is a case of ' having the word on the tip of one's tongue ' (otherwise one could not be sure it exists), but the search for it illustrates well enough the sense of linguistic interactions indispensable to a writer.

> The process of writing a poem – in many instances – consists of cajoling an unbodied something into its incarnation. . . . Before it has found itself in words by finding the words for itself, that *something else* has as little character, is as little describable as a name we are trying to recall.[63]

I. A. Richards, poet as well as critic, knows the process from inside. To reach wholly beyond linguistic convention is impossible, but the temptation is always there in a creative writer : the temptation of those ' interstices ' which are growing points in individual perception and also perhaps in the slowly changing system as a whole. Provided the gap across which the writer reaches is not too great, the reader will be able to cross it with him.[64] As J. R. Firth, one of the first linguists to take a fruitful interest in stylistics, wrote,

There is the element of habit, custom, tradition, the element
of the past, and the element of innovation, of the moment,
in which the future is being born. When you speak you fuse
these elements in verbal creation, the outcome of your
language and your personality.[65] What you say may be said
to have style, and in this connection a vast field of research in
stylistics awaits investigation in literature and speech.[66]

Clearly, to be as aware as it is possible for one person to become
of the matrix of the language is the only honest course for the
reader, especially if he is also a critic. He must be able not only
to respond to the work in terms of that matrix and the possibilities it offers (in order to know whether they have been well
exploited), but also to convey to others, in clear explanatory
terms, what would otherwise seem a matter of unverifiable, even
if convincing, intuition. If he is also a teacher, this requirement
becomes a duty: students are to be taught rather than (however brilliantly) brainwashed. But these points I have already
made, briefly, in the introduction. Unless what we describe is
capable of being felt intuitively, there would be no point in
describing it. On the other hand, to the extent that we cannot
describe it, we cannot share our experience with others. Nor can
we build up, in our culture, that understanding of verbal art
which might provide a larger audience responsive to good writing.
Verbal art is surely the least understood of all, probably because
its material is so familiar and yet so deeply internalised that it is
scarcely perceived. Perhaps a wider realisation of how strange
a medium *all* language is will help us to break through those
inhibitions that prevent our studying verbal art as we would
any other.[67]

Linguistic theories, techniques and descriptions are no insult
to the mystery of language. They are largely responsible for our
new awareness of it. And they are the best means we have of
studying the phenomenon adequately because, as Firth said,
linguistics 'separates from the mush of general goings-on those
features of repeated events which appear to be parts of a pat-
terned process, and handles them systematically by stating them
by the spectrum of linguistic techniques' so that it proceeds 'by
a method rather like the dispersing of light of mixed waves into
a spectrum':

Descriptive linguistics is thus a sort of hierarchy of techniques by means of which the meaning of linguistic events may be, as it were, dispersed in a spectrum of specialised statements.[68]

The study of literature and of language should always be, from the earliest years, a form of active research, not the static learning of facts. At undergraduate level, the student's exploration can, at this stage in the development of stylistics, add not merely to his or her own knowledge, but to the general sum of what is known.

The Individual

The problem that faces the creative writer, then, is essentially that which faces us all. We all have to use the 'blue guitar' of language so as to express things 'exactly as they are' in our immediate experience: that is, as they do *not*, through the medium of ordinary language, appear to be.

> People living at the seashore grow so accustomed to the murmur of the waves that they never hear it. By the same token, we scarcely ever hear the words we utter. . . . We look at each other, but we do not see each other anymore. Our perception of the world has withered away, what has remained is mere recognition.[69]

Shklovsky was right. Well handled or meaningfully departed from, the conventions of natural language can rescue human awareness from automation. And this, no doubt, has a most important role to play in human survival as well as personal development. Henry Miller's conception of the importance of 'language' as against isolated words finds confirmation in modern linguistics as it would not have in earlier periods of language-study. In language, in writing, as Miller says, 'one can only go forwards by going backward and then sideways and then up and then down. There is no progress: there is perpetual movement, displacement, which is circular, spiral, endless' or, as Sapir wrote, 'the possibilities of individual expression are infinite, language in particular is the most fluid of mediums' even though language is a system 'où tout se tient'. Charles Davy has speculated that, just as a chess-player may well have an inner vision of 'the purely abstract pattern of force-relations' at any one point in a game, so in the writing and reading of a poem, there might be such relational perceptions at work.

> In poetry the pattern becomes more complex, involving the sounds of words and their symbolic meanings, but one may suppose that it *could* be brought before the inner sight. . . . It would be much richer than a chess-relations-pattern, and also (unless a few words were focussed in isolation) it would not be static, but changing continually while the poem was heard or read.[70]

Responding to a poem, or to prose, is a matter of responding both to the external relations of the text (to a language-structure and to culture) and to internal structural processes. Many writers have said that, while composing, they have a sense of a shape or movement to be actualised. In my own experience, success in finding the right word, rhythm or syntactical form can feel like nothing so much as a lid slipping down into place on a screw-top jar! Unromantic as that image may make the process appear, the experience is satisfying to an extraordinary degree (as, no doubt, finding *the* word was for Valéry). What the writer senses is not some platonic essence resisting embodiment but relational possibilities (formal and semantic) which the poem, if it is successful, *does* embody, the writer having sensed the potentiality for them and succeeded in their actualisation. Like a single word we may be trying to recall (to use Richards's metaphor), the whole shape of a poem is already waiting to be found in the 'spirals' of the language-system.

Writers have attempted to describe the act of creation in varying ways. This is Shelley:

> Poetry is not like reasoning, a power to be exerted according to the determination of the will. A man cannot say, 'I will compose poetry'. The greatest poet even cannot say it; for the mind in creation is as a fading coal, which some invisible influence, like an inconstant wind, awakens to transitory brightness; this power arises from within, like the colour of a flower which fades and changes as it is developed, and the conscious portions of our natures are unprophetic either of its approach or of its departure. Could this influence be durable

in its original purity and force, it is impossible to predict the greatness of the results; but when composition begins, inspiration is already on the decline, and the most glorious poetry that has ever been communicated to the world is probably a feeble shadow of the original conceptions of the poet.[71]

From this it would seem that Shelley's habit was to begin actual composition too late, rather than trust verbalisation 'on the page' from the beginning, in the way Richards describes. The Russian poet and novelist Pasternak, on the other hand, recreates as follows the experience of his fictional Dr Zhivago in the process of writing poetry, and this description lacks all suggestion of a 'fading coal'.

After two or three stanzas and several images by which he was himself astonished, his work took possession of him and he experienced the approach of what is called inspiration. At such moments the correlation of the forces controlling the artist is, as it were, stood on its head. The ascendancy is no longer with the artist or the state of mind which he is trying to express, but with language, his instrument of expression. Language, the home and dwelling of beauty and meaning, itself begins to think and speak for man and wholly turns into music, not in the sense of outward, audible sounds but by virtue of the power and momentum of its inward flow. Then, like the current of a mighty river polishing stones and turning wheels by its very movement, the flow of speech creates in passing, by the force of its own laws, rhyme and rhythm and the countless other forms and formations, still more important and until now undiscovered, unconsidered and unnamed.[72]

This description supports Shklovsky when he says 'it seems obvious to me that for a writer words are not a necessary evil, or merely the means of saying something, but the very material of the work. Literature is made up of words and is governed by the laws that govern language.' It is not so surprising to find Dylan Thomas, surely the opposite of a dry pedant, saying:

To your third question – do I deliberately utilise devices of rhyme, rhythm, and word-formation in my writing – I must, of course, answer with an immediate 'Yes'. I am a painstaking, conscientious, involved and devious craftsman in words, however unsuccessful the result so often appears, and to whatever wrong uses I may apply my technical paraphernalia. I use everything and anything to make my poems work and move in the direction I want them to: old tricks, new tricks, puns, portmanteau-words, paradox, allusion, paronomasia, paragram, catachresis, slang, assonantal rhymes, vowel rhymes, sprung rhythm. Every device there is in language is there to be used if you will. Poets have got to enjoy themselves sometimes, and the twistings and convolutions of words, the inventions and contrivances, are all part of the joy that is part of the painful voluntary work.[73]

To come back, now, to the questions with which I began this chapter: there is nothing trivial in the exploration of how language works, much less in the exploration of how it works in literature. In truly creative language, we share someone else's discovery of what Jung called 'the very edge of the world'.

Only the man who is modern in our meaning of the term really lives in the present; he alone has a present-day consciousness, and he alone finds that the ways of life which correspond to earlier levels pall upon him. The values and strivings of those past worlds no longer interest him save from the historical standpoint. Thus he has become 'unhistorical' in the deepest sense and has estranged himself from the mass of men who live entirely within the bounds of tradition. Indeed, he is completely modern only when he has come to the very edge of the world, leaving behind him all that has been discarded and outgrown, and acknowledging that he stands before a void out of which all things may grow.[74]

Here, Shelley's 'void' and Miller's arrival at 'the brink' meet in a new significance.[75] But a writer in this situation re-establishes his link with mankind, through language. For him, in the words of Gabriel Marcel, 'my experience is in a real communication with other experiences. I cannot be cut off from one without being cut off from the other.'[76]

Our understanding of literature must involve the interrelationship of forms and meanings in unique wholes in which, more or less completely, the accidents of language have been redeemed. These wholes are not made up merely of sequences of linguistic events, which have a 'shape' thanks only to their occurrence.

They are structures in which some elements, that might dominate in a different structure, are subordinated to others, because of their function in the whole.[77] The good writer (like a musician) organises our field of perception sequentially, as the painter organises our perception of a plane surface. It seems likely that, at least in stylistic analysis that takes account of the influence of meaning, the better the work, in this sense, the more closely different readers' descriptions of its dominant structures will agree,[78] because these will be 'stable' in the sense often used of what perceptual psychologists call 'good' visual figures. This is speculative. But we can at least be sure that Nietzsche's view of the role of what he called 'philology' applies fruitfully to modern linguistics.

> I have not been a philologist in vain; perhaps I am one yet: a teacher of slow reading. I even come to write slowly. At present it is not only my habit, but even my taste, a perverted taste, maybe – to write nothing but what will drive to despair everyone who is in a hurry . . . philology is now more desirable than ever before; . . . it is the highest attraction and incitement in an age of 'work': that is to say, of haste, of unseemly and immoderate hurry-scurry, which is intent upon 'getting things done' at once, even every book, whether old or new. Philology itself, perhaps, will not 'get things done' so hurriedly: it teaches how to read *well*: slowly, profoundly, attentively, prudently, with inner thoughts, with the mental doors ajar, with delicate fingers and eyes . . . .[79]

Chapter II

Anyone who doubts the inseparability of form and meaning cannot do better than attempt the translation even of quite ordinary utterances.[1] Most of us have experience of this, so I shall concentrate instead on the special problems of literary translation. Something general has already been said about these in the previous chapter. It remains to explore a particular text.

I have chosen Paul Valéry's *Les Pas*. We have already seen some of Valéry's thoughts about writing, which show him to have been a conscious craftsman. The translation is by the English poet, C. Day Lewis. Its inadequacy illustrates much more than a personal failure on Day Lewis's part: it illustrates a failure in translation-theory as applied to literature, which in turn reflects a weakness of literary criticism which the stylistics of dominant form could do something to correct. Just what is meant by dominant form will emerge more clearly in the next chapter. For the moment, the reader will see for himself that *Les Pas* is, in what follows, approached as a unit, a unit with certain dominant features which are so vital to its meaning and perceptual outline that translation must, to be faithful in any worthwhile way, work on the basis of a prior stylistic analysis of them. This Day Lewis clearly did not do, and his version distorts quite unnecessarily essential features of the original, as well as losing others which any translator would find difficult to imitate or substitute for. As Sapir wrote:

> The literary artist may never be quite conscious of just how much he is hindered or helped or otherwise guided by the matrix, but when it is a question of translating his work into another language, the nature of the original matrix manifests itself at once. All his effects have been calculated, or intuitively

felt, with reference to the formal ' genius ' of his own language; they cannot be carried over without loss or modification.[2]

In other words, the better the writer handles the medium, the harder he or she will be to translate, though this is the opposite of what is often said. In making decisions as to what to attempt to preserve or parallel, the translator should work, I believe, not with general precepts – as, for example, that syntax is vital, or connotation – but with his eye on each individual structure, whether it be prose or verse. Each structure will lay stress on certain linguistic features or levels and not on others, and it must be treated as a unique communicative whole. The point is the same as that made about the interpretation of deviant features (which themselves will, of course, feature prominently amongst the translator's problems). If the reader will bear this in mind when he reads the next two chapters, on verse and prose, he will see what wide-ranging consequences such a principle might well have on the translation of the texts explored, and how easily its absence might lead to the distortion of vital communicative aspects of the original.

Reference to the texts[3] printed on facing pages 44 and 45[4] will show that several prominent features of *Les Pas* fail to reappear in *The Footsteps*. And, moreover, that the English poem has a less marked and relevant structure than the original French poem, so that we cannot say Day Lewis has created an alternative, equally well-formed poem whose tenuous relations with the original might be forgotten in favour of its intrinsic value. Let us explore both poems in some detail.

Les Pas starts and ends with phrases that echo the title, *tes pas* and *vos pas*. And these phrases reveal another essential feature, the change from the intimate *tes* to the more formal *vos*, the opposite direction of change from what one might expect in what seems to be some sort of love-poem. The poem arcs between these two points, and any understanding of it must solve the puzzle they pose. The change is very sudden, and comes in the last sentence, which begins with the familiar form and ends with the formal, the last two lines of the last verse being the crisis-point (my italics):

> Ne *hâte* pas cet acte tendre,
> Douceur d'être et de n'être pas,
> Car j'ai vécu de *vous* attendre,
> Et mon cœur n'était que *vos* pas.

It is here, too, that the only archaism appears, *car*, with *de n'être pas* the only inverted phrase, so that the last verse carries some poetic weight, and this hint is confirmed by its meaning, since it is here that we discover that the person who advances towards his bed so deeply affects the poet that not only is he in a state of 'being and not being', but he has 'lived by awaiting' her and his heart was 'nothing but' her steps. Her? It is a subtlety of the poem that it avoids any gender, being addressed to a 'you' who is never described save by actions and effects. The nature of this person is very carefully balanced also between 'being and not being': *personne pure, ombre divine*, the substantiality of *personne* being countered by *ombre*. Again, the (apparently human) lips of verse 3 prepare, for the 'inhabitant of my thoughts', *la nourriture d'un baiser*, the 'food' of a 'kiss' which clearly has metaphysical as well as material connotations. This balance stretches throughout the poem. Verse 2 has the ambiguous *dons* (like the English *gifts* meaning both 'presents' and artistic gifts) being brought 'on bare feet', reviving the human aspect of the theme: and yet these feet were first described abstractedly as 'children of my silence'. And indeed when we consider the connotations of the words used in the poem, we see that many are religious: *saintement, vigilence, pure, ombre, divine, Dieux, dons*, even perhaps *devine*. It seems the poem is based on the metaphor of a lovers' meeting, the woman coming to the man's bed, but has to do, at another level, with some divine visitation, perhaps of the muse, but the muse understood as the deepest desire of the poet's thoughts, the source of his life, identifiable with the beat of his heart or rather with his heart itself: *mon cœur n'était que vos pas*. The change to the formal mode of address reflects the seriousness of the encounter and perhaps that subtle fear in the poet's ecstasy which leads him to doubt the coming kiss (*si . . . tu prépares*) and to wish its postponement (*ne hâte pas*). It seems that the kiss may also mean death, since the steps are the heart. It is an essential aspect of the poem's effect that, after the first two neatly-rhymed verses, with their relatively short sentences, verses 3 and 4 contain just one long, hypothetical sentence, with the dependent clause first, the wish for postponement at its centre as the main clause, and the clause which brings us nearest to the significance of the whole concluding the poem on a note of suspended realisation. It is also an essential, and related, feature that the poem is entirely in the present tense – in view of its subject, it must be.

Les Pas

Tes pas, enfants de mon silence,
Saintement, lentement placés,
Vers le lit de ma vigilence
Procèdent muets et glacés.

Personne pure, ombre divine,
Qu'ils sont doux, tes pas retenus!
Dieux!... tous les dons que je devine
Viennent à moi sur ces pieds nus!

Si, de tes lèvres avancées,
Tu prépares, pour l'apaiser,
A l'habitant de mes pensées
La nourriture d'un baiser,

Ne hâte pas cet acte tendre,
Douceur d'être et de n'être pas,
Car j'ai vécu de vous attendre,
Et mon cœur n'était que vos pas.[3]

The Footsteps

Born of my voiceless time, your steps
Slowly, ecstatically advance:
Towards my expectation's bed
They move in a hushed, ice-clear trance.

Pure being, shadow-shape divine –
Your step deliberate, how sweet!
God! – every gift I have imagined
Comes to me on those naked feet.

If so be your offered mouth
Is shaped already to appease
That which occupies my thought
With the live substance of a kiss,

Oh hasten not this loving act,
Rapture where self and not-self meet:
My life has been the awaiting you,
Your footfall was my own heart's beat.[4]

What does Day Lewis make of this? Let us look at *The Footsteps* in the same order as *Les Pas*. The English version loses the placing of the phrases at opposite ends of the poem, unnecessarily since *your steps* and *your footfall* might have been placed as the French phrases are. And why compound the loss by varying the lexis? And having yet another variant for the title! The important change from familiar to formal is lost too. Although that is one of those linguistic features that belong to the ' original matrix ', in view of its thematic importance some substitute should surely have been found : some indication of the change of attitude is necessary to any poem claiming to translate *Les Pas*. The last verse of *The Footsteps* fails, then, to capture this effect, and the poem as a whole shows an insensitivity to Valéry's use of familiar and archaic language. So *car* is not represented at all in the last verse, the last two lines being in fact more colloquial than many others. Elsewhere we have *if so be* and *Oh hasten not*, which have no register-equivalents in Valéry who, as we saw, keeps such obvious poetic turns for the last verse, and even when they come they are less showy. Much of the rest of the language is noticeably simple, serving to set off the close. Day Lewis preserves without difficulty the non-identification of the approaching figure as man or woman, but fails to catch the oscillation between human and immaterial that is a feature of Valéry's phrasing. *Personne* is changed to *being,* with its ethereal connotations, while *ombre* is made more concrete by its alteration to *shadow-shape* : so twice getting the wrong effect. *Nourriture*, similarly, becomes *live substance*, losing the ambiguity of the French (and adding some extraneous notions), and the materiality of *l'habitant de mes pensées* becomes the cliché abstraction *that which occupies my thought* (why not *thoughts*, with its implication of more complete involvement?). *Dons* is caught in *gift* (though again in the singular), only to fail in its effect by being followed by *imagined*, whose implications are quite different from those of *devine* (one can imagine something that is not there, one ' devines ' the presence of a reality). *Naked feet*, too, translates *pieds nus* well enough, but *born of my voiceless time*, describing the origins of the footsteps, is fussy, less concrete (*enfants/born*) and semantically a poor rendering of *enfants de mon silence*, which conveys the possibility of deliberate silence, not mere *voicelessness* – which brings us to the religious aspect of the poem's lexis. These are Day Lewis's equivalents :

saintement	ecstatically
vigilence	expectation
pure	pure
ombre	shadow-shape
divine	divine
Dieux	God
dons	gift
devine	imagined

Without *shape*, *shadow* would have had the same connotations as *ombre*, with it these are attenuated at least, if not banished. The pagan touch of *Dieux* is dropped (and yet it is important to the poem in so far as the figure may be the muse). *Ecstatically* and *expectation* replace two of the most important adjectival clues to the poem's subject, and replace them by an emphasis on the lovers' meeting interpretation. *Trance*, an addition, scarcely makes up for these losses. Not surprisingly, the rendering of the last verse reflects this failure : *where self and not self meet* in no sense reproduces *douceur d'être et de n'être pas*, and is open to total misinterpretation (as a reference to the lovers' meeting instead of to an internal ontological experience). The penultimate line misses a crucial implication – that the poet's life has been not ' spent in ' waiting but ' derived from ' waiting – and the final identification of the steps with the heart itself, rather than just the heart-beat (and thus with all the emotive implications associated in French, as in English, with the heart). But at this point it becomes evident that to trace in further detail Day Lewis's departures from *Les Pas* is becoming unnecessary – the English poem has already failed in too many essentials. We have only to conclude by noticing that the two-verse sentence, too, has been reorganised, and with it the effects of suspense (so beautiful in Valéry) largely destroyed. Compare :

Si ...	If so be your offered mouth
Tu prépares ...	Is shaped ... to appease
...	That which occupies my thought
La nourriture d'un baiser,	...
Ne hâte pas ...	O hasten not ...
...	...
Car j'ai vécu ...	My life ...
Et mon cœur ...	Your footfall ...

I hope the reader, following the two texts, will see how the interjections of the French are overridden in the English and independent sentences introduced at the end, breaking the articulated flow of the concluding dependent clauses. Moreover, the semantic emphasis falls quite differently, not on 'preparation' and 'nourishment' but on the mouth, its shape, 'appeasement' and the occupant of the poet's thoughts. For that matter, the change of order in the final line, placing *your footsteps* where they should not be, at the beginning of the line, also distorts the semantic emphasis, 'my heart was your steps' becoming 'your steps were my heart ('s beat)'. The whole notion of an outside influence is thus diminished, since now the meaning can be that the poet realises the steps he has heard are really his heart beating, whereas Valéry's more fearful meaning is the reverse, that what the poet thought was his heart was really the walking of the divine shadow. The last comment that seems worth making is that although Day Lewis begins with the present tense, he changes, for no relevant effect, to the past in line 3 of verse 1, thus introducing a sense of time passing into a poem which is, in the original, suspended in a moment of time almost outside time : *douceur d'être et de n'être pas*, an eternal present threatened by the desired and feared metaphysical kiss.

The changes in Day Lewis's translation are not to be excused on the grounds of rhyme, in view of the vagueness of his scheme :

1	2	3	4
steps	divine	mouth	act
advance	sweet	appease	meet
bed	imagined	thought	you
trance	feet	kiss	beat

In some cases, greater exactitude would have produced better rhyme, for example *divine* or even *imagine* in verse 2. As an English poem, *The Footsteps* is undistinguished – as I think it is unnecessary to demonstrate separately after what has been said about its semantic inconsistencies and structural weakness : the reader will see that little or nothing has been added that could provide an alternative structure or a consistent new meaning. The poem is a case of perceptual 'bad form'. It gives the impression of having been inaccurately translated *ad hoc*, in terms of words, word-clusters, lines, but never in terms of the whole.[5] It is in fact, despite its inaccuracies, analytically rather than synthetically conceived.

The blame for this cannot fairly be laid at the individual translator's door. A distinguished poet in his own right, Day Lewis was working without an adequate theory of literary translation. Abandoning the kind of word-by-word faithfulness that many lesser translators might have aimed for, he has nevertheless not taken into account the relation of parts to each other and to the whole. Valéry's poem is a structural unit with dominant traits essential to its identity. Whatever might have to be lost in translation, those traits should have been preserved, or replaced by others that could function similarly. Put another way, the criteria of selection that guided this translation are inadequate and inconsistent. The effort, such as it is, that went into preserving some vestiges of the rhyme-scheme, for example, might have been better employed on matters which, *in this poem*, are more important. In another poem, rhyme might have been vital. What is needed is a description of the dominant structure of every individual work to be translated.[6] This is not a recipe for looseness in translation, although literal translation at word-level might have to be sacrificed in order to achieve more important effects. It is a recipe for the kind of accuracy that matters most, that which will preserve the original as a communicative act and perceptual unit within the limits imposed by the new matrix.

Chapter III

We can begin discussing some of the practical implications of looking closely at formal-semantic relations with this short poem by Arthur Waley, translated from the Chinese.

> Swiftly the years, beyond recall.
> Solemn the stillness of this spring morning.[1]

Critics have found these lines effective. William Empson's is perhaps the classical account, and it is of particular interest to us since it comes in *Seven Types of Ambiguity*, one of the foundation-texts of modern close criticism. It is worth quoting entire, both for its value and for what it leaves out, despite its length.

> The human mind has two main scales on which to measure time. The large one takes the length of a human life as its unit, so that there is nothing to be done about life, it is of an animal dignity and simplicity, and must be regarded from a peaceable and fatalistic point of view. The small one takes as its unit the conscious moment, and it is from this that you consider the neighbouring space, an activity of the will, delicacies of social tone, and your personality. The scales are so far apart as almost to give the effect of defining two dimensions; they do not come into contact because what is too large to be conceived by the one is still too small to be conceived by the other. Thus, taking the units as a century and the quarter of a second, their ratio is ten to the tenth and their mean is the standard working day; or taking the smaller one as five minutes, their mean is the whole of summer. The repose and self-command given by the use of the first are

contrasted with the speed at which it shows the years to be passing from you, and therefore with the fear of death; the fever and multiplicity of life, as known by the use of the second, are contrasted with the calm of the external space of which it gives consciousness, with the absolute or extra-temporal value attached to the brief moments of self-know-ledge with which it is concerned, and with a sense of security in that it makes death so far off.

Both these time-scales and their contrasts are included by these two lines in a single act of apprehension, because of the words *swift* and *still*. Being contradictory as they stand, they demand to be conceived in different ways; we are enabled, therefore, to meet the open skies with an answering stability of self-knowledge; to meet the brevity of human life with an ironical sense that it is morning and springtime, that there is a whole summer before winter, a whole day before night.

I call *swift* and *still* here ambiguous, though each is meant to be referred to one particular time-scale, because between them they put two time-scales into the reader's mind in a single act of apprehension. But these scales, being both present, are in some degree used for each adjective, so that the words are ambiguous in a more direct sense; the *years* of a man's life seem *swift* even on the small scale, like the mist from the mountains which 'gathers a moment, then scatters'; the *morning* seems *still* even on the large scale, so that this moment is apocalyptic and a type of heaven.

Lacking rhyme, metre, and any overt device such as com-parison, these lines are what we should normally call poetry only by virtue of their compactness; two statements are made as if they were connected, and the reader is forced to consider their relations for himself. The reason why these facts should have been selected for a poem is left for him to invent; he will invent a variety of reasons and order them in his own mind. This, I think, is the essential fact about the poetical use of language.[2]

These comments illuminate the semantic workings of the poem. But do they account for its perceptual effect? Donald Davie brings us nearer, I think, when (in the course of a comment on Hugh Kenner's treatment of the lines) he says 'What are missing are the verbs, hence the syntax.'[3] Davie is pointing here to a crucial aspect of structure. We can rewrite the lines either as

> Swiftly fly the years, beyond recall.
> Solemn is the stillness of this spring morning.

or

> Swift the years, beyond recall.
> Solemn the stillness of this spring morning.

And although Empson's comments still apply, the original effect of the poem has evaporated. Why? In the first rewritten version, two verbs have been introduced, in the second an adverb has been changed. The most obvious result is that the lines are no longer syntactically deviant. Even the second version is now a sequence of two *acceptable* elliptical forms (' Lovely, this weather '). But we have to go beyond this, of course, to explain why rewriting the poem in these ways destroys much of its effect. After all, it does not seem that Davie would think so. In his view, the verbs are ' missing ' , not just absent: he goes on to remark that ' where the verbs *should be* ' (my italics) we have a ' yawning vagueness '. His attention is focused on the workings of metaphor, rather than on this poem in particular, so it is no criticism to say that, despite his greater closeness to the text, his comments, like Empson's, fail to do the poem justice. The clue, probably, is the assumption that the syntax is missing because the verbs are. On the contrary, what we have is a skilful use of syntax to mime the meaning. Line 1 is ' incomplete ' in a sense not applicable to line 2. The adverb *swiftly* leads us to expect a verb, a verb which could still appear after *beyond recall* (read aloud, the intonation should preserve that possibility). The second line therefore breaks in upon line 1, as if line 1 were short of time, and in its completeness it represents time stilled instead of snatched away. Moreover, the elliptical form, a syntactical equivalent of an initial ' how ', provides intensity and immediacy of effect, supporting the contrast of *the years* to *this . . . morning* (with its demonstrative). Certainly not irrelevant here is the fact that, when we fill in the verbs, the likeliest verbs for line 1 are verbs of action, ' fly ', ' pass ', ' go ', while the most likely verb for line 2 is the verb ' be ', not action but existence. The perceptual effect of Waley's poem depends not (not only) on the ideas it appeals to but on the way the language works as a linguistic *event*. ' It is not with ideas that one makes sonnets, it is with words ', as Mallarmé admonished the painter Degas when the latter brought him some of his efforts in verbal art. The syntax is not missing, it is being used – to better effect than if the verbs that 'should be there' *had* been there. The meaning, as it is carried into our minds by the language, is live beyond anything Empson's commentary accounts for or Davie's would allow. The meaning is not just described, it happens. And that, whether it involves deviation or not, is what *using* language is all about. 'A poem should not mean, but be' is perhaps another (though a misleading) way of indicating this.

Literary criticism has offered, at various times, prescriptions for good writing, especially for good poetry, which advocate particular kinds of linguistic usage. Leavis's preference for 'local life', 'fusion', 'sensuous particularity', Empson's stress on 'ambiguity', Davie's on 'purity of diction', these are modern examples and each has yielded positive critical results in certain areas and made us think harder about how language works.[4] Stylistics, however, if it is prescriptive at all, should be so only in a wider sense, adopting a functional view, one that will accommodate any usage that *works as communication*. This is the only way to do justice to the past and the future (the only basis, too, for an adequate approach to creative writing courses, one of the most important applications of literary stylistics).[5] One has only to think how ill Leavis's criteria apply, for example, to the great French poet Racine to realise that they are improperly restrictive. How do we know that such a writer will not arise in English, only to meet barriers of incomprehension (such as Racine does in fact meet in many British readers)? Or, if the example of Racine seems inappropriate because of the language difference, we have only to look at Leavis's treatment of the later Milton[6] to see that he has missed many of Milton's virtues through too exclusive an application of certain standards of excellence. It may be interesting to see how these standards, backed up by inadequate technical means, lead Leavis to mis-analyse the passage from *Paradise Lost* on which he has chosen to base his argument against the later style. First, the passage:

> The hasty multitude
> Admiring enter'd, and the work some praise
> And some the Architect : his hand was known
> In Heav'n by many a Towred structure high,
> Where Scepter'd Angels held their residence,
> And sat as Princes, whom the supreme King
> Exalted to such power, and gave to rule,

> Each in his Hierarchie, the Orders bright.
> Nor was his name unheard or unador'd
> In ancient Greece; and in Ausonian land
> Men called him Mulciber; and how he fell
> From Heav'n, they fabl'd, thrown by angry Jove
> Sheer o'er the Chrystal Battlements : from Morn
> To Noon he fell, from Noon to dewy Eve,
> A Summers day; and with the setting Sun
> Dropt from the Zenith like a falling Star,
> On Lemnos th' Aegæan Ile : thus they relate,
> Erring . . .[7]

Leavis's comment is as follows.

The opening exhibits the usual heavy rhythmic pattern, the hieratic stylisation, the swaying ritual movement back and forth, the steep cadences. . . . But from ' Nor was his name unheard ' onwards the effect changes. One no longer feels oneself carried along, resigned or protesting, by an automatic ritual, . . . the verse seems suddenly to have come to life. Yet the pattern remains the same; there are the same heavy stresses, the same rhythmic gestures, and the same cadences, and if one thought a graph of the verse-movement worth drawing it would not show the difference. The change of feeling cannot at first be related to any point of form; it comes in with ' ancient Greece ' and ' Ausonian land ', and seems to be immediately due to the evocation of that serene, clear, ideally remote classical world so potent upon Milton's sensibility. But what is most important to note is that the heavy stresses, the characteristic cadences, turns, and returns of the verse, have here a peculiar felicity. What would elsewhere have been the routine thump of ' Sheer ' and ' Dropt ' is here, in either case, obviously functional, and the other rhythmic features of the verse are correspondingly appropriate. The stress given by the end-position to the first ' fell ', with the accompanying pause, in what looks like a common, limply pompous Miltonicism –

> and how he fell
> From Heav'n, they fabl'd, thrown . . .

– is here uncommonly right; the heavy ' thrown ' is right, and so are the following rise and fall, the slopes and curves, of the verse.[8]

One must assume that Leavis had studied the verse-movement in more detail than he gives here and had found it unchanging throughout. This led him to seek the cause of the change, which he felt intuitively, in a change of function: the *same* verse-movement changes from inappropriate to appropriate, that is his explanation. A closer look reveals other changes, however, changes in the verse-movement itself. Here is the passage again, with sentence, clause and group boundaries marked. (The arrows at the end of some lines will be explained in the commentary.)

```
 1          ///The hasty multitude《
 2   Admiring》enter'd, //and/the work/some/praise//
 3   And/some/the Architect://his hand/was known/→
 4   In Heav'n/by many a Towred structure high,//
 5   Where/Scepter'd Angels/held/their residence,//
 6   And/sat/as Princes,//whom/the supreme King/→
 7   Exalted/to such power,//and/gave/to rule,《
 8   Each/in his Hierarchie,》the Orders bright.///
 9   Nor/was/his name/unheard or unador'd/→
10   In ancient Greece;//and/in Ausonian land/⟫
11   Men/called/him/Mulciber;//and⟦how/he/fell/⟫⟫
12   From Heav'n,⟧they/fabl'd,//thrown/by angry Jove/→
13   Sheer o'er the Chrystal Battlements://from Morn ⟫
14   To Noon/he/fell,/from Noon to dewy Eve,⟫
15   A Summers day;//and/with the setting Sun/⟫
16   Dropt/from the Zenith/like a falling Star,/→
17   On Lemnos th' Aegæan Ile:///thus/they/relate,//
18   Erring...⁹
```

The interesting thing, here, is that where a clause-boundary does not coincide with a line-end, in the opening section of the passage, a group-boundary *does* occur and is reinforced by the interjection of an adjunct, *in Heav'n* (line 4), or is semantically justified by emphatic stress, *exalted to such power* (line 7), the point being that their power is given by God, the eventual challenge to his divinity being the more shameful. Apart from these two exceptions, lines 1–8 are consistently end-stopped, and from line 9 onwards the reverse is the case. The run-on between lines 9 and 10 is, however, of the type we saw between lines 3 and 4, *in ancient Greece* acting, like *in Heav'n*, to *reinforce* a pause. But after this, the pattern changes. The adjuncts come at the ends of lines instead of at the beginning, so that by the end of the line we are again being pulled *forward*. This is the case in lines 10–11 with *in Ausonian land*, 12–13 with *by angry Jove*, 15–16 with *with the setting Sun*, and also in 16–17, though here the case is a little more complex and requires a word of explanation : *like a falling star* parallels the other adjuncts in its line-end position, and the following adjunct, though not absolutely required by the syntax, is made likely by the verb, since things usually drop *to* as well as *from* somewhere, so that we are again drawn forward. In lines 11–12 the syntactical pull is strong, since the line-end occurs within a rankshifted object ('and *this* they fabl'd ') and one which in its inverted position directs the reader strongly forward towards the subject and verb to follow. In lines 13–14 the break comes within a group, again, and in lines 14–15 within a group of a more complex kind, since *a Summers day* is in apposition to *from Noon to dewy Eve*. The verse-movement is thus more complex than a quick glance at the line-ends would lead one to suspect. With lines 17–18, the end-stopping recurs, as befits the subject-matter.

To summarise : single-headed arrows mark the occurrence of run-on of a relatively weak sort over a group-boundary, double-headed arrows run-on where syntactical features tend to draw the reader (or listener) forward, and double-shafted arrows where run-on occurs within a group. It would be difficult, having examined the passage closely, to deny the accuracy of Leavis's intuition on the one hand or, on the other, the inadequacy of the method of analysis which led him to miss the subtle formal change. A graph of the verse-movement *is* worth drawing, and it does show the difference.

All this may not be very exciting, but it is a safe bet that Milton would have preferred a judgement based on what he wrote.[10] The verse-movement of the earlier part of the passage seems to be well-adapted to its subject, the architectural and hierarchical features of Heaven and Hell being figured in the observance of line-unit controls, just as the later handling of the verse is functionally related to Mulciber's fall. Milton might, in fact, be praised for his *variation* of verse-movement, and for the functional use to which he puts it in *both* parts of the passage.[11] And this, of course, is in direct opposition to Leavis's conclusion. Leavis is so great a critic that a slip of this kind, in a crucial passage of one of his major essays, must make us realise that the true fault lies with the critical tradition, a point which is validated by the fact that his analysis has been so widely accepted for so long. We need better tools of analysis as well as more comprehensive and undogmatic theories as to the workings of language if we are to establish a reliable and sensitive discipline. It is a pity that when modern British criticism was laying its foundations in the early years of the century, it had to break away from a form of philology which threatened to stifle it.[12] Modern linguistics also broke away from that philology, and at much the same time. The irony is that the two younger disciplines have not yet recognised each other as allies. We are only at the beginning.

Let us look again now at that short poem by Robert Graves, *Flying Crooked*. It will be helpful in clarifying some issues related to deviation and its role in poetic language.

> The butterfly, the cabbage-white,
> (His honest idiocy of flight)
> Will never now, it is too late,
> Master the art of flying straight,
> Yet has – who knows so well as I? –
> A just sense of how not to fly:
> He lurches here and here by guess
> And God and hope and hopelessness.
> Even the aerobatic swift
> Has not his flying-crooked gift.[13]

The poetic form is regular octosyllabic couplets. After line 4, even the syntax falls into two-line units coinciding with the rhymes. The syntax internal to this pattern, though, is quite different: not literary but colloquial, accommodating deviation as well as much interruption. Other features contribute to an erratic effect, so that all are best considered together. In fact the only marked touch of literariness in the diction occurs with the inversion *has not* and the compound adjective *flying-crooked*, both in the last line, which thus deviates from the poem's own norms and brings the conclusion to the fore.

The appositional structure of line 1, more marked by the use of the second *the* than it would have been by the use of *a*, is followed by a group of words in line 2 which have no assignable relation to the sentence and are thus syntactically abnormal, as against *langue*, although we can assume that their meaning is something like 'thanks to his honest idiocy of flight'. Line 3 harks back to the subject in line 1, provides part of the verbal group, *Will never*, interrupts it with the adjunct *now* and the clause *it is too late*. The rest of the verbal group appears in line 5 and the remainder of that line runs forward smoothly (as the meaning dictates, perhaps). Then we are off again on an erratic course, the verb *has* being separated from its object *A just sense of how not to fly* by two clauses, *who knows* (this) *so well as I* (do). The object itself is semantically odd, since we usually have a just sense of how to *do* something, not of how *not* to do it. *Lurches* is lexically deviant, applied to a light body like a butterfly. *Here and here* is so unusual that many readers spontaneously read it as 'here and there'. The only normal usage of the phrase that Graves actually chose would be if the speaker were present in a situation, pointing out the butterfly's movements to someone present with him. *Here and here* could then refer to separate spots. Despite the present tense of the poem, however, there is nothing to suggest such immediacy: it is *the* (not this) *butterfly* – cabbage-whites in general – and the *is* seems to represent a state of affairs. We must, I think, take it that the phrase depicts the lurching of the butterfly from and back to the *same* spot (a realistic flight-pattern). Since the idiom is distorted, the reader also 'lurches', expecting to go forward and being brought back by the second *here*. The phrase thus has a mimetic role. 'By guess and by God' (normally with the second *by*) is another fixed phrase partially distorted here, since it plainly has its original meaning, 'by trial and error', but also each lexical item carries some of its separate meaning, revived by the continuation of the line with *and hope and hopelessness*. The relationship of the four items seems, at first, a mirror-image one (not the simplest pattern), but on consideration of the poem as a whole, one is inclined to associate *guess* with *hope*, and *God* with *hopelessness* after all: the poet clearly prefers the 'crooked' to the 'straight' way, and guessing to certainty. The last two lines run easily at last and contain the assured decision that 'the gift of flying crooked' is preferable to *the art of flying straight*, the two phrases (in their different forms) echoing each other across the poem so that the opening clause, stating the theme, is rounded off by the last. The last line also, as we have seen, contains the only literary diction in the poem, which seems to emphasise that this is a *poet's* last word!

The poem neatly opposes erratic internal syntax to the regularities of the octosyllabic couplet, as if to say ' Here I am writing all crooked, how clumsy, like the butterfly – but then, I get the octosyllabics just right. Quite a gift, really. And come to that, the lurching is pretty well-controlled, too, wouldn't you say?' That is surely the implication also of *who knows so well as I*? The poem is a moral epigram, in just the accepted overall poetic form, but reversing the accepted *internal* form, and morality. It makes cleverer use of formal-semantic contrast than we find in another of Graves's poems, where instead of opposing two types of form, he opposes only form and meaning.[14] The poem is called *In Broken Images*.

> He is quick, thinking in clear images;
> I am slow, thinking in broken images.
>
> He becomes dull, trusting to his clear images;
> I become sharp, mistrusting my broken images.
>
> Trusting his images, he assumes their relevance;
> Mistrusting my images, I question their relevance.
>
> Assuming their relevance, he assumes the fact;
> Questioning their relevance, I question the fact.
>
> When the fact fails him, he questions his senses;
> When the fact fails me, I approve my senses.
>
> He continues quick and dull in his clear images;
> I continue slow and sharp in my broken images.
>
> He in a new confusion of his understanding;
> I in a new understanding of my confusion.[15]

And the syllogistic structure proves it!

Returning now to a more analytical approach, we have to consider how norms and deviations from norms entered into our impressions of *Flying Crooked*. Clearly, they did enter into my explanation of the poem's effects. Equally clearly, the way in which such impressions are picked up is by no means easy to explain. Jan Mukařovský, in his discussion of *Standard Language and Poetic Language*,[16] concludes ' it is possible in some cases for a component which is foregrounded in terms of the norms of the standard, not to be foregrounded in a certain work because it is in accord with the automatised poetic cannon '. A little later, he goes on:

The background which we perceive behind the work of poetry as consisting of the unforegrounded components resisting foregrounding is thus dual: the norm of the standard language and the traditional esthetic cannon. Both backgrounds are always potentially present, though one of them will predominate in the concrete case.[17]

Now, even leaving aside the appeal to only two potential backgrounds, this seems quite inadequate to account for the effects of the poem we have been looking at (not, surely, a particularly complex work). We seemed to grasp some features against two backgrounds at once. Thus the octosyllabics may perhaps, on an initial reading, fall into the background, being seen as normal in terms of the poetic cannon. But by the time we have fully grasped the poem, the poetic form is brought to the foreground of attention by the relevance it has as a signal of competent poetic handling and as an ironic comment on the epigrammatic moralising tradition. At this point, then, we grasp it both in relation to the poetic norms *and* in relation to the standard language (that is, the colloquial standard), since we savour simultaneously its *positive appeal to* the octosyllabic tradition and its foregrounding *against speech*-norms, represented in the poem by an internal syntax which, in its turn, is foregrounded against the *poetic norm*. Thus both norms appear to be present, perceptually, and neither, in *this* concrete case at least, predominates.

No doubt thinking in terms of background and foreground, as one might do in the case of simple visual figures, can be misleading. The analogy has further drawbacks, which appear when Mukařovský writes

> . . . the simultaneous foregrounding of all components of a work of poetry is unthinkable. This is because the foregrounding of a component implies precisely its being placed in the foreground; the unit in the foreground, however, occupies this position by comparison with another unit or units that remain in the background. A simultaneous foregrounding would thus bring all components onto the same plane and so become a new automatization.[18]

This must seem true if we consider a simple figure-ground model (see Figure 3); even if the figure-ground relationship is reversible, the black and the white figures cannot be foregrounded *simultaneously*.

Fig. 3.

But, in Figure 3 at least, the foregrounding occurs in relation to elements *present* in the drawing. In poetry (and in figures like that on page 32), foregrounding by deviation or by other means may, and often does, occur in relation to norms established *outside* the work. And if different norms can be held simultaneously against the poem, in the perceptual mind's-eye, as seemed to be happening with *Flying Crooked*, it seems theoretically possible also for all elements of a work to be foregrounded simultaneously, even against ' clashing ' norms.

Finally, before we turn to the longer studies, a major issue remains to be touched on. In my comments on Waley's poem, the Milton passage and *Flying Crooked* I have assumed that the relevance of form to meaning is a crucial issue. It would seem, indeed, essential to the process not only of description – since relevance or the reverse may influence perceptual prominence – but also for evaluation, since we tend to feel that functional uses of language are superior to non-functional (as in Leavis's and my own discussions of Milton). It is therefore interesting to consider an opposing view. This is Mukařovský's unambiguous statement of an extreme formalist (if not typically Formalist) position.

> In poetic language foregrounding achieves maximum intensity to the extent of pushing communication into the background as the objective of expression and of being used for its own sake; it is not used in the services of communication, but in order to place in the foreground the act of expression, the act of speech itself.[19]

The assumption behind this is, no doubt, that the aesthetic use of a medium means its non-utilitarian use. On this theory, the 'use' of language is communication: therefore, its aesthetic exploitation must imply its *non*-use for communication. This is no place to take up major issues of aesthetics. But one notices a difficulty. There is, in Mukařovský's scheme, no way of assessing the success of poetic language other than by its degree of fore-grounding (foregrounding being associated exclusively, by him, with deviation, although that is certainly not an adequate inter-pretation).[20] Poetic language aims at what he calls 'the maxi-mum of foregrounding'. But if we consider how far this mode of assessment would tally with that which we instinctively employ, we foresee ludicrous results. Swinburne would come higher in the new canon than Shakespeare, and we should have no means of accounting for our delight in normal but appropriate language or our distaste for purposeless linguistic distortion. It is hard to believe that the reader's everyday 'set towards the message' (his spontaneous search for meaningfulness) could be so strangely reversed when it comes to poetry, or any other sort of language-use. More plausible to assume, on the contrary, that the intensity of his concentration on meaningfulness is increased, that he looks more deeply into the structure of the act of speech, seeking more and more subtle clues as to its communicative value, especially since literary language comes to him isolated from situational clues.[21] Linguistic form gets more attention in the close reading of literature not because it draws attention to itself and away from meaning but because it functions more relevantly than usual in relation to meaning and so becomes a focus of semantic curiosity.

It is on this assumption that the following studies proceed. Although we shall have to solve problems of analysis intuitively – adequate research in many areas still remaining to be done – we can at least bear in mind several related points. Dominance or 'foregrounding' is not necessarily, as we have seen, dependent on deviation from any norm:[22] it may be dependent on positive appeal to the norm, or on semantic appropriateness. Deviation itself can be assessed against various norms, notably those of *langue, parole*, the poetic tradition, the work itself (all these being capable of subdivision, and one could expand the list):[23] the reader must attend, as Nietzsche says, 'with delicate fingers and eyes'. Moreover, it seems that more than one norm may be per-ceptually active in a single reading, even if they conflict (as do the norms of the standard language and of the poetic tradition).

D. H. Lawrence's *Gloire de Dijon* is interesting as an example
of (almost) free verse. An insensitive reaction might be that it
'has no form', but it is in fact a striking example of the truth
of Eliot's remark, 'No verse is free for the man who wants to do
a good job'.[24] Lawrence did a good job, and it was a job he had
thought a great deal about, as we shall see when we consider
his comments on the nature and *raison d'être* of free verse. The
poem also allows us to pick up the point that dominance or
'foregrounding' is not necessarily a matter of deviation. *Gloire
de Dijon* owes little to deviation and a great deal to appropriateness, though the two interact in a particularly charming way
to create the dominant structure.

1   When she rises in the morning,
2   I linger to watch her;
3   She spreads the bath-cloth underneath the window
4   And the sunbeams catch her
5   Glistening white on the shoulders,
6   While down her sides the mellow
7   Golden shadow glows as
8   She stoops to the sponge, and her swung breasts
9   Sway like full-blown yellow
10   Gloire de Dijon roses.

1   She drips herself with water, and her shoulders
2   Glisten as silver, they crumple up
3   Like wet and falling roses, and I listen
4   For the sluicing of their rain-dishevelled petals.
5   In the window full of sunlight
6   Concentrates her golden shadow
7   Fold on fold, until it glows as
8   Mellow as the glory roses.[25]

The first reading of the poem leaves an impression of light, direct
(white, silver) and indirect (the gold of the shadow, allied with
the yellow of the roses). So even shadow is given in terms of
light. The relationship of the woman to the 'I' of the poem is
indicated in the first two lines, by the syntax, which suggests
habitual delight in watching her (*When she rises in the morning,
I...*), and by *linger*, which conveys a lover's reluctance to leave.
As the light-imagery emphasises throughout the poem, the visual

point-of-view is within the room : the woman is seen against the light, with direct sunlight striking only her shoulders, the rest of her body bathed in glowing shadow, much like the woman in Degas's pastel of 1886, ' The Tub '.[26] (The parallel is indeed so close that I have wondered whether Lawrence the painter had this pastel in mind when he wrote the poem.)

In line 3 the first of a series of line-initial phrases occurs, all depicting the woman's actions : *She spreads . . ., She stoops . . .* (verse 1, line 8), *She drips herself . . .* (verse 2, line 1). This series concludes with a new ' actor ', *her golden shadow*, the subject-verb relation inverted and *Concentrates her golden shadow* occupying the whole of verse 2, line 6.[27] This contains, as it were, the ' story ' of the poem : the woman as actor being taken over by her shadow, merging through it almost completely with the image of the rose – elsewhere, her breasts sway like full-blown roses, her shoulders *crumple up/Like wet and falling roses* and she has *rain-dishevelled petals* until finally her shadow concentrates *fold on fold*, like a rose. The taking-over of her active role, figured in the syntax, is only the completion of the process, an increasing but instantaneous intensity in which time seems to flow slowly : one notices the distance separating *She drips herself* from *I listen/For . . .*, and still the water has not fallen.

This provides an outline within which to study more subtle effects. We can already see that the poem repeats and intensifies certain features of the scene, building up in each verse to the image of the roses which provide the poem's title. The first two lines seem to stand aside as a ' frame ', they do not enter fully into the chain of the woman's actions, since *she rises* occurs in a dependent clause and not at the beginning of the line, that position being occupied by the subject-verb of the main clause, *I linger*.[28] How do the details support this view?

Reading through the lines in sequence, we reach the first full rhyme[29] with *mellow*, which tells us that *window* in line 3 was a rhyme.[30] The off-rhyme *watch her . . . catch her* (lines 1 and 4) influences us to expect a rhyme either for *morning* or *window*, an expectation *shoulders* (line 5) disappoints, so that when it comes *mellow* receives particular emphasis. Immediately after *mellow* we have the first run-on, and a strong one, between two adjectives in the same nominal group. And the rhyme-vowel, /əʊ/, recurs in every lexical item of the following line, with no intervening grammatical items, so that we have a powerful auditory sequence ' mell*ow* g*o*lden shad*ow* gl*ow*s ' brought to the fore by rhyme and by run-on, not to mention the fact that we have here the key image of the poem,[31] the *golden shadow*, itself lexically unusual (shadows are usually, though not of course always accurately, described as dark and nearly always in terms of a 'cool' colour of the spectrum, for example blue or green). For several reasons, then, the group of words containing the repeated sound are perceptually prominent. As we read on, we can be expected to notice the recurrence of the words involved and of the sound itself, so let us set out (in order of appearance) both the lexical items that recur and the words that contain / əʊ /, many receiving the emphasis of line-end positioning.

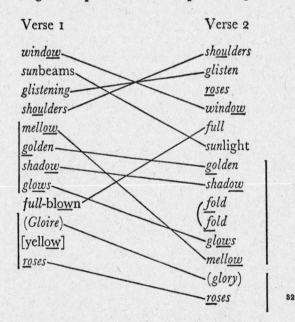

	Verse 1	Verse 2
	window	*sh*ou*lders*
	sunbeams	*glisten*
	glistening	*r*o*ses*
	shoulders	*wind*ow
	*mell*ow	*full*
	*g*o*lden*	*sunlight*
	*shad*ow	*g*o*lden*
	*gl*ow*s*	*shad*ow
	*full-bl*ow*n*	*fold*
	(Gloire)	*fold*
	[*yell*ow]	*gl*ow*s*
	*r*o*ses*	*mell*ow
		(glory)
		*r*o*ses* [32]

No items are repeated within verse 1, verse 2 thus receiving the full impact of the device. It is noticeable that the opening of verse 2 contains the opening lexical series of verse 1, and that the series *mellow golden shadow glows* recurs unbroken (save for *fold on fold* which is a repetition unique to verse 2 having, here, the effect of intensifying the impression of the surrounding items), though *mellow* now comes at the end of the group rather than at the beginning. Two other items, the cross-language *Gloire/glory* and *roses* (the only item occurring three times), appear as a group at the end of each verse. Apart from these repeated items, there are a number of others containing / əʊ /, including the only two items repeated within a verse, *roses* and *fold*. The items containing / əʊ / could, indeed, almost be said to summarise the visual theme : *window, shoulders, mellow, golden, shadow, glows, full-blown, yellow, roses, fold*. (Only two of these are not repeated, *blown* and *yellow* : the first is closely associated with *full*, while *yellow* is echoed phonologically and semantically in *golden*, which is also repeated.[33]) The circular intensification of the visual comes out best when we take the full sequence of lexico-phonological repetitions as Lawrence introduces it in the poem :

verse 1   window, shoulders, mellow, golden, shadow, glows, full-blown, roses;

verse 2   shoulders, roses, window, golden, shadow, fold, fold, glows, mellow, roses.

To this must be added the intensifying shift from *white* (direct light on her dry shoulders) to *silver* (direct light on her wet shoulders), the deviation from normal syntax in *She drips herself* (again, an intensifying reflexive), the move from simile (verse 1) to metaphor (verse 2, lines 1–4), and the take-over of the shadow from the woman which we have already discussed, and which involves an inversion which places the verb *Concentrates* and the subject which follows in stressed positions thus emphasising precisely the relevant meanings by creating a delicate ambiguity between voluntary concentration and intensification as by a natural process. (It is worth noticing the visual accuracy of the most extravagant image, that of the shoulders ' crumpling up ' : water dripped on to the shoulders does in fact break up into patches before running off, though this is another rapid effect which, thus noticed and described, contributes to the impression of slow motion at this point in the poem.)

Looking back over the poem as a whole, one can see that the opening two lines do introduce the rest, and stand outside two series of eight lines (verse 1, lines 3–10 and the whole of verse 2) starting with the line that contains the first repeated *and* first / əʊ / item, *window*.[34]

Lawrence has written a poem that revives the ancient association of the beloved with the rose, but he has made the woman stand for the rose as much as the rose does for the woman. And because he has introduced the observer so explicitly – and reminds us of his presence again in verse 2 – we are aware that his theme

implies an attitude towards love itself : love, not as possession, but
as mutual singleness, as many other poems tell us. And this is how
he describes free verse :

> . . . there is another kind of poetry : the poetry of that which
> is at hand : the immediate present. In the immediate present
> there is no perfection, no consummation, nothing finished.
> The strands are all flying, quivering, intermingling into the
> web, the waters are shaking the moon. . . .
> Life, the ever-present, knows no finality, no finished crystal-
> lization. The perfect rose is only a running flame, emerging
> and flowing off, and never in any sense at rest, static, finished.
> Herein lies its transcendent loveliness.[35]

Gloire de Dijon combines intensity with continuous movement;
even at the end there is no stasis, everything is in the present tense
and the concentration is a process, slowed down only by the
abnormally keen attention of a human eye. The whole situation,
by its nature, is a passing one : a woman washing in the morning, a man about to leave but lingering a moment, in Lawrence's
words ' the quality of life itself, without denouement or close '.

> Much has been written about free verse. But all that can be
> said, first and last, is that free verse is, or should be, direct
> utterance from the instant, whole man. It is the soul and the
> mind and body surging together, nothing left out. They speak
> all together. There is some confusion, some discord. But the
> confusion and discord only belong to the reality, as noise
> belongs to the plunge of water. It is no use inventing fancy
> laws for free verse, no use drawing a melodic line which all
> feet must toe.

The images that occur in the poem tend to occur in Lawrence's
writings about free verse, the rose, the water and its noise, elsewhere ' the momentous association of things which meet and
pass on the ever incalculable journey of creation; everything
left in its own rapid fluid relationship with the rest of things '.
Which is only to say that the poem seems to match his ideals,
both as to poetic form and as to subject-matter, exactly. In order
to grasp its form analysis must be without prejudices as to what
poetic form *should* be : it must be ready to recognise whatever
is there, whatever functions to create the effect. Free verse, as

Lawrence said, 'has its own nature . . . instantaneous like plasma'. That does not mean it is critically ungraspable nor that it is carelessly put together, simply that each poem will have a form of its own because 'for such utterance any externally applied law would be mere shackles and death. The law must come new each time from within.'

> Such is the rare new poetry. One realm we have never conquered: the pure present. One great mystery of time is *terra incognita* to us: the instant. The most superb mystery we have hardly recognised: the immediate, instant self. The quick of all time is in the instant.

What these comments make clear, whether we agree with Lawrence or not, is that the choice of poetic form is always conditioned by more than the immediate subject. It is conditioned, also, by fundamental metaphysical biases and preoccupations in the writer and perhaps in his time. In this sense, the medium may be a large part of the message.

Looking back on *Gloire de Dijon*, one can see how prominence is achieved for certain effects by co-operating devices. Repetition would be tedious. The reader will see for himself that various kinds of deviation, together with recurrences of sound that can hardly be classed as deviation, focus attention on crucial features of the poem and contribute not only to its 'shape' (2 + 8 + 8 lines) but also to the overall concentration of effect. The prominence of certain words and of / əʊ /in verse 1 trigger off a perceptual slant which draws attention, in what follows, to other / əʊ / items as well as to the most important image, that which makes the 'bridge' between the woman and the roses. As items begin to repeat, in verse 2, so other modes of intensification are brought into play. The result is a form, a unique form, appropriate to the meaning, largely avoiding linguistic regularity but exploiting linguistic potentials.

Interacting features and lexical repetition also play a part in *The Falcon* (or *Corpus Christi Carol*). The poem is otherwise as different from *Gloire de Dijon* as it could be, with its traditional rhyme-scheme and refrain and its highly formalised, if unique, chain of lexical repetitions. For the purpose of this study, I have assumed that the refrain recurs after every verse, and this assumption marginally affects the description of the poem's dominant structure.

1   *Lully, lulley! Lully, lulley!*
    The faucon hath borne my make away!

2   He bare him up, he bare him down,
    He bare him into an orchard brown.

    Lully, lulley! Lully, lulley!
    The faucon hath borne my make away!

3   In that orchard there was an halle,
    That was hanged with purple and pall.

    Lully lulley! Lully, lulley!
    The faucon hath borne my make away!

4   And in that hall there was a bed,
    It was hanged with gold so red.

    Lully, lulley! Lully, lulley!
    The faucon hath borne my make away!

5   And in that bed there li'th a knight,
    His woundes bleeding day and night.

    Lully, lulley! Lully, lulley!
    The faucon hath borne my make away!

6   At that bed's foot there li'th a hound,
    Licking the blood as it runs down.

    Lully, lulley! Lully, lulley!
    The faucon hath borne my make away!

7   By that bed-side kneeleth a may,
    And she weepeth both night and day.

    Lully, lulley! Lully, lulley!
    The faucon hath borne my make away!

8   And at that bed's head standeth a stone,
    Corpus Christi written thereon.

    Lully, lulley! Lully, lulley!
    The faucon hath borne my make away![36]

The speaking voice in this poem is of interest because it plays a
dual role: first as the voice, one assumes, of the poet or singer
of the carol, then as the voice of the maid weeping at the bed-
side *within* the poem. This effect is reinforced, when the refrain

is repeated after each verse, by the fact that only with verse 7 do verse and refrain rhyme, the first two lines of the verse being also the only other vowel-rhyming lines in the poem. It is perhaps not irrelevant, especially if we imagine the carol sung, that the vowel in question is one easily lending itself to a cry of lament. A further point to be made about the refrain is that its implication changes in the final verse. Until then, since the lament appears to be for a human being, we interpret the falcon as an image for death, which has brought the beloved to the knight's deathbed. When we know the knight is Christ, we know he will arise from the bed – that is, from the tomb (verse 8, line 1) – and the falcon can perhaps be seen now as bearing the beloved toward his saviour and eternal life (and therefore only temporarily away from the singer). The falcon appears as the normal accompaniment of a knight (like the faithful hound and the weeping maid) but the anonymous writer seems to be drawing, too, on the same ancient well of imagery from which Gerard Manley Hopkins drew his windhover, the 'dapple-dawn-drawn falcon', symbol of Christ's ultimate overcoming of death.

Following the poem through from verse 1 (later to be the refrain), we are led forward by a chain of lexical repetition, which can be shown as on page 71. The opening repetitions *borne-bare-bare-bare* emphasise the central narrative event and launch the repetitive chain. The following three repetitions follow the pattern set by the last two *bare*'s, taking us down to verse 5. Here, the pattern alters, and instead of a new lexical item, we get the exhaustion of the possibilities of compounds with *bed*: *bed's foot*, *bed-side*, *bed's head*. The *bed*-chain reaches a crisis there, since there is no further possibility for expansion, and there the poem does in fact come to an end.

So far as lexical repetition is concerned, then, *The Falcon*'s structure lays emphasis on the notion of 'bearing away' (important thematically, as we have seen) and then draws us forward to the central point, the bed, on which the knight, Christ, lies. But we do not yet know this is Christ, and after the 'zoom-in', the camera pans round, as it were, to take in relevant aspects of the central scene, freezing on the crucial stone which almost simultaneously tells us we are looking not at a bed but at a grave (i.e. that the poem is metaphorical) and that the occupant is Christ whose *woundes* bleed *day and night* for mankind, the blood of sacrifice and of redemption. That is why, of course, the tense changes to the present in verse 5, with the discovery of

Verse 1

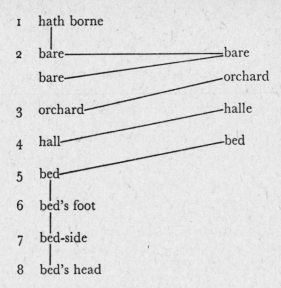

1 hath borne

2 bare —————————— bare
   bare ————————— orchard

3 orchard ——————— halle

4 hall ———————— bed

5 bed

6 bed's foot

7 bed-side

8 bed's head

the body : ' this is always so ', even if the vision of it (recorded in the poem) is in time and is past by the time it can be communicated. And the refrain's *hath borne* fits easily with either tense. The present tense also serves, no doubt, another purpose, that of making the scene more immediate to us. The *that*'s preceding *bed's foot*, *bed-side* and *bed's head* are subtly different from those which, before, merely indicated previous reference : now, they can serve also as demonstratives.[37]

The poem as a whole reaches a crisis in verse 5, where the lexical pattern changes and the tense becomes present. The knight is introduced, and we are then led forward, by a different kind of lexical chain, to the discovery of his identity, and therefore of the significance of the maid's weeping and the lament of the poem as a whole : in verse 7, the voice of a figure within the poem joins that of the singer of the carol, mourning within mourning, and the refrain rhymes with the verse, while in verse 8 the headstone reveals the poem's true subject, simultaneously altering the refrain's emotional connotations and bringing the poem satisfactorily to a close at the conclusion of a limited lexical chain. The mourners grieve together and are comforted together.

The prominence of the lexical chain is guaranteed by regularity and simplicity, which make us notice it where more sporadic repetition might pass unnoticed (not being unusual in speech). The prominence of the verse-refrain rhyme is made more perceptible than it might otherwise be by the absence of vowel verse-rhyme elsewhere (so that the *may* and *day* of verse 7 break a norm of the poem), and most significantly by the semantic relevance of the quadruple rhyme at this point in the narrative.[38] This is surely a good analogy for the dot becoming prominent when it is seen as the rabbit's nose: if the rhyme of verse with refrain played no semantic role, the description of the poem's dominant structure would need to take no special notice of it, since its perceptual prominence would be minimal – which is a forcible reminder of the fact that description is selection, and that selection-criteria cannot plausibly be considered to be merely formal in all cases.

The last poem we shall discuss is one which is even more intricate in its structure than those we have been looking at, and yet which appears simple. It is one of the lyrics from Tennyson's *The Princess*, and a close study of it reveals a meaning which is not, I think, clear at first sight, and was perhaps not intended to be.

1   Now sleeps the crimson petal, now the white;
     Nor waves the cypress in the palace walk;
     Nor winks the gold fin in the porphyry font:
     The firefly wakens: waken thou with me.

2   Now droops the milkwhite peacock like a ghost,
     And like a ghost she glimmers on to me.

3   Now lies the Earth all Danaë to the stars,
     And all thy heart lies open unto me.

4   Now slides the shining meteor on, and leaves
     A shining furrow, as thy thoughts in me.

5   Now folds the lily all her sweetness up,
     And slips into the bosom of the lake:
     So fold thyself, my dearest, thou, and slip
     Into my bosom and be lost in me.[39]

These fourteen lines are divided so that the first and last verses

have four lines and the middle three two each. Each verse begins
with the pattern *Now* + *verb* (third person present tense) + *the*,
each item taking up a single syllable. The last line of each verse
ends with a *preposition* + *me*, and the preposition always
suggests movement ' towards ' rather than ' away from ': *with me*,
to me, *unto me*, *in me*, *in me*, the last two being particularly
insistent in their repetition of *in*. The verses are thus well marked
even though they are not structured by rhyme. Intervening lines
echo the pattern of opening lines to some extent, the whole result
being best shown by abstracting the features concerned.

1   Now sleeps the . . .
            Nor waves the . . .
            Nor winks the . . .
            . . . with me.

2   Now droops the . . .
            . . . to me.

3   Now lies the . . .
            . . . unto me.

4   Now slides the . . .
            . . . in me.

5   Now folds the . . .
            And slips . . .
            So fold . . .
            . . . in me.

Something is worth adding about the verbs that enter this pattern. In verses 1–3, these verbs are either passive *in meaning* and
grammatically positive, or active *in meaning* and grammatically
negative. So *sleeps*, *droops* and *lies* are positive, and *waves* and
winks negative. With verse 4 this changes, *slides* being (in contrast to the first series) active in meaning and also positive grammatically, and the same can be said of *fold*, *slip* and *fold*. It is
also noticeable that there is an alternating relationship between
the verbs from verse 4 onwards: *slides*, *fold*, *slips*, *fold*, the first
and third being related in meaning and sound, the second and
fourth being the same item. It is too early yet to say what effect
this may have in the poem as a whole, but the general impression
is one of increased activity from the beginning of verse 4. Does
anything else support that impression?

If we consider the line-final items, we notice that up to the end of verse 3, all are in some sense nominal: they are either nouns or pronouns (the pronouns being, in each case, of course, within adjunct-groups). The first line of verse 4 breaks this pattern, with the line-final verb *leaves*, and thereafter each alternate line-end item is a verbal item, *up* (from *fold up*) and *slip*. And these verbal items themselves alternately coincide with the only run-ons in the poem, in the first line of verse 4 and the third of verse 5. Alternation was, we remember, a feature of the verbal chain *slides*, *fold*, *slips*, *fold*, and we can bear this in mind as we go on accumulating further detail. The main point here is that the break in the unusual line-end monotony of nominal items (generally to be shunned in traditional English poetry) comes in the first line of verse 4, as does the first run-on. And we have not only a break but a *significant* one for the notion of movement, since it is caused (precisely) by the introduction of a verb and of run-on, both obviously associated with movement, an impression reinforced by the meaning of the verb chosen, *leaves*. What, then, can we say about the motivation of this change, partially concealed as it must surely be for most readers on a first reading by the stability of certain other, repeated, elements?[40]

First, the two invocations to the beloved. Looked at side by side they seem contradictory.

> The fire-fly wakens: waken thou with me.

> So fold thyself, my dearest, thou, and slip
> Into my bosom and be lost in me.

Apart from the greater urgency of the second (rendered chiefly by *thyself*, *my dearest*, *thou*), there is an important difference. The first asks her to waken, like the firefly but unlike vegetable nature, but the second asks her to withdraw, like the lily, and so fall in with vegetable nature. She is not to wake all night like the firefly but to slip away like the lily. Is this a mere contradiction, a bit of poetic nonsense excusable in a Victorian lyric of which we do not dare demand very high standards of cogency? It would be a pity to jump to conclusions before we have discussed the metaphors rather closely.

The woman is first asked to liken herself to the firefly. She is then likened to the Earth which lies open to the sky as Danaë lay open to the golden shower (of which the stars are a further metaphor) of Jove. The reference is explicitly sexual here, and the lover is associated with Jove and thus with the stars. Now the thoughts of the woman (not herself, we notice) are likened to a meteor, so that, in her turn, she is associated with the cosmos, by means of an image which surpasses the potency of the stars and which, because of the reference to a *furrow* also has (traditional) sexual connotations (usually reserved for men, as in Shakespeare's usage). Finally, she is likened to a lily, at which point the lover metaphorically becomes the lake into which she slips. All this argues a reversal of roles. In verse 3, the lover's call has clearly succeeded, his beloved has come to him. His role is the traditional active role of the male, to whom the woman is ' open '. In verse 4, the firefly image is incredibly answered by that of the meteor, and now the woman's thoughts traverse the lover's inner consciousness like a meteor traversing the passive sky. And finally, returning to the natural landscape, the beloved is a lily slipping into the lake of the lover's bosom, with its connotations of care and protection, a meeting of the two types of metaphor since both lovers, now, are quiescent.

If this is the case, the *now*'s indicate different points in time, not one point, and the poem traces a progression in which there is an unspoken hiatus, between verse 3 and verse 4, and here the love is consummated and the lovers' roles are reversed, though his active role was physical and hers is spiritual. The transformation is indicated not only in the features we have looked at already, but also in the discreet *on* of verse 4, line 1 (one moves on *from* something) and in the transformation of the landscape, the petals and font of verse 1 being replaced by the lily and lake of verse 5, the final scene containing the same elements but subtly sweeter and more wild, a metamorphosis appropriate to being ' lost ' (verse 5) in love.

And metamorphosis is the deep theme of the poem, despite its initial air of stability. The myth of Danaë was aptly chosen. The alternating patterns that appear in the poem from verse 4 onwards have some bearing on this : one senses the greater flexibility of the structures, and the regularity of alternation itself, as a contribution to a changed, more flowing, emotional rhythm.[41]

Chapter IV

Much prose, too, shows effects that are describable entirely or partly in terms of linguistic detail.[1] So let us look at a number of short passages which, without in any way illustrating the full range of structural possibilities, will serve as a background for the discussion of a single short story, D. H. Lawrence's *The Blind Man* (printed in its entirety on pages 112–129 below). The reader may consider how easily many of the effects discussed might be lost in translation, if a careful stylistic analysis were not first carried out. This, in turn, will make clear how greatly the communicative impact of the passages, and of the story, depend on features of language that might well escape critical attention, especially in prose – although we saw in the case of Waley's short poem that they often enough escape notice in poetry too.

As in the last chapter, my focus is on the whole communicative act, and I do not undertake, therefore, a general description (or 'grammar') of traits of style, though the information derived from such descriptions might feed into the type of study undertaken here,[2] especially if they include analyses of recurrent narrative *motifs* in the manner of Todorov's studies on the Decameron stories.[3] It might be found, for example, that the impact of a certain passage in a given story had much to do not merely with its own internal structure but with its deviation from the author's usual narrative method, assuming the reader to be familiar with that method. Not only the stories of such writers as Ambrose Bierce and Somerset Maugham might be worth looking at from this point of view, but also more complex stories, those of Hemingway, of Faulkner and of D. H. Lawrence amongst others. However, this would take us beyond the scope of this book.

Here are two passages from Conrad's *The Secret Agent.*

1   The Chief Inspector, steady-eyed, nodded briefly his comprehension, and opened the door. Mrs Verloc, behind the counter, might have heard but did not see his departure, pursued by the aggressive clatter of the bell. She sat at her post of duty behind the counter. She sat rigidly erect in the chair with two dirty pink pieces of paper lying spread at her feet. The palms of her hands were pressed convulsively to her face, with the tips of the fingers contracted against the forehead, as though the skin had been a mask which she was ready to tear off violently. The perfect immobility of her pose expressed the agitation of rage and despair, all the potential violence of tragic passions, better than any shallow display of shrieks, with the beating of a distracted head against the walls, could have done. Chief Inspector Heat, crossing the shop at his busy, swinging pace, gave her only a cursory glance. And when the cracked bell ceased to tremble on its curved ribbon of steel nothing stirred near Mrs Verloc, as if her attitude had the locking power of a spell.[4]

2   He saw partly on the ceiling and partly on the wall the moving shadow of an arm with a clenched hand holding a carving knife. It flickered up and down. Its movements were leisurely. They were leisurely enough for Mr Verloc to recognise the limb and the weapon.

They were leisurely enough for him to take in the full meaning of the portent, and to taste the flavour of death rising in his gorge. His wife had gone raving mad – murdering mad. They were leisurely enough for the first paralysing effect of this discovery to pass away before a resolute determination to come out victorious from the ghastly struggle with that armed lunatic. They were leisurely enough for Mr Verloc to elaborate a plan of defence involving a dash behind the table, and the felling of the woman to the ground with a heavy wooden chair. But they were not leisurely enough to allow Mr Verloc the time to move either hand or foot. The knife was already planted in his breast.[5]

In the first passage, we have the description of a crisis in Mrs

Verloc's life. She had married to provide a home for her mentally-deficient brother, Stevie, and has just overheard the Chief Inspector telling her husband about his death. This death, though accidental, has occurred in a manner which is particularly horrifying, and in circumstances which lay the blame at Mr Verloc's door. The Inspector has been speaking in an inner room of the shop, opens the door into the shop, walks through (past Mrs Verloc) and out by the street door with its cracked bell. How does Conrad convey Mrs Verloc's state of shock?

One aspect of his handling comes out clearly if we change the verbal elements in his second description of the Inspector's departure:

> Chief Inspector Heat, as he crossed (or *had crossed*) the shop at his busy, swinging pace, had given her only a cursory glance. And when the cracked bell had ceased to tremble on its curved ribbon of steel nothing had stirred near Mrs Verloc, as if her attitude had (or *had had*) the locking power of a spell.

What Conrad did, as against what this rewritten passage does, was to deviate from the sequence of tenses that would be expected in the context. After all, Inspector Heat has already left once: and on the first occasion, we do not even see him go, he has already gone (sentence 2). When Conrad returns to him, he describes his departure as if it were only now taking place, so not just repeating the incident but actually taking a step backward in time before the original account of it. The technique is cinematographic, it communicates a backward overlap in time, not merely immobility or recurrence, which mimes very adequately a certain psychological impression often present in states of shock. Many readers will know Ambrose Bierce's short story about a hanging during the American civil war, *An Occurrence at Owl Creek Bridge*,[6] and will remember the passage at the end where the escaping man repeatedly runs forward into the clearing where he sees his wife waiting for him, only to be snatched inexplicably back, until we suddenly realise that we have been witnessing the escape-fantasy of a man dropping on the hangman's rope, finally to be snatched back into death. In the film that was made of this story, an overlapping technique was used much like that (to jump from the excellent to the ridiculous) which, in an advertisement few cinema-goers can have missed, renders the notion of endless, entrancing ecstasy while consuming a bar of Crunchie (no doubt, in the latter case, the technique also has sexual undertones – or overtones). The time-slip effect in the Conrad passage is only one aspect of its structure, however. The sentence describing Mrs Verloc's immobile posture is worth a close look.

> The palms of her hands were pressed convulsively to her face, with the tips of the fingers contracted against the forehead, as though the skin had been a mask which she was ready to tear off violently.

Consider these phrases in sequence (my italics):

> the palms of *her* hands
> *her* face
> the tips of *the* fingers
> *the* forehead
> *the* skin
> *a mask*

There is an increasing depersonalisation of Mrs Verloc's body, from *her hands* and *her face*, to *the fingers* and *the forehead*, emphasised by *the skin* (semantically, a ' surface' feature) and culminating in *a mask*, something totally divorced from the self. Conrad is exploiting a feature of the language which would not be at his disposal in French, since French normally employs impersonal forms for parts of the body: a variation could be introduced superficially similar to this one, but it could not have the same perceptual effect. As R. L. Stevenson said, ' the deviation of . . . phrases from their so-called natural order is luminous for the mind '.

In the first passage, then, two devices, one basically narrative but involving the deviant use of tense-sequences, the other wholly a matter of linguistic detail, co-operate to bring meaning alive in perceptual terms. The second passage is not altogether unlike it and again involves a time-slip, as must be evident even on a first reading. However, the details are of great interest.

The first sentence begins a process which is prolonged through the passage. It delays recognition of the semantically relevant features of what Mr Verloc sees, imitating his shock and slowness of mind:

He saw . . . partly . . . on the ceiling . . . and partly . . . on the wall . . . the moving shadow . . . of an arm . . . with a clenched hand . . . holding a carving knife.

It is noticeable that the nouns get more and more specific, *shadow . . . arm . . . clenched hand . . . carving knife.* The next sentence picks up the hint of *partly on the ceiling and partly on the wall* with *It flickered up and down.* In other words, Mrs Verloc is not just moving towards her husband, knife in hand – she is in the process of striking, the knife must be about to slide home. The movement is a rapid one: *It flickered.* But now the process is held up by a chain of similar sentences, and the similarity extends beyond the obvious *Its movements/They* plus *were leisurely.*

Its movements were	leisurely	to . . .
They were	leisurely enough for . . .	
They were	leisurely enough for . . . to . . .	

. . . .

They were	leisurely enough for . . . to . . .	
They were	leisurely enough for . . . to . . .	
But they were not	leisurely enough	to . . .

The break in the pattern comes with the sentence *His wife had gone raving mad – murdering mad,* the moment at which Verloc realises what has happened. The other sentences, after the first two, are prolonged in such a way as to emphasise the impression of there being time for elaboration, whether of subjective feelings or plans of escape. *But . . . not* ushers in a change, however. And this is followed by a gap in the expected syntactical pattern: we go straight from *enough* to the *to . . .* construction, an omission which is all the more striking for the ease with which the established pattern might have been adhered to: ' But they were not leisurely enough *for* Mr Verloc *to* recognise . . .'. We find ourselves further along in the sentence than we might have expected, and by the time we read the next sentence we see the relevance of this effect, since *The knife was already planted in his breast. Already planted* indicates that we never witness the strike itself, not even to the extent that would have been indicated, for example, by *The knife had already struck his breast. Planted* is far more final, stiller. The moment of death has occurred somewhere before, in the midst of Verloc's thoughts, so that Conrad reproduces for us, if we follow him, the sense of impotence and shock which, in this instance, he does not directly describe. And he does it largely by means of subtle detail framed within what must be counted rather obvious devices.

It may be interesting to compare this with another manipulation of time, by Dickens in *Oliver Twist*. Here, the reader's time is brought into play as well as the prisoner Fagin's.

He sat down on a stone bench opposite the door, which served for seat and bedstead : and casting his blood-shot eyes upon the ground, tried to collect his thoughts. After a while, he began to remember a few disjointed fragments of what the judge had said : though it had seemed to him, at the time, that he could not hear a word. These gradually fell into their proper places, and by degrees suggested more : so that in a little time he had the whole, almost as it was delivered. To be hanged by the neck, till he was dead – that was the end. To be hanged by the neck till he was dead.

As it came on very dark, he began to think of all the men he had known who had died upon the scaffold; some of them through his means. They rose up, in such quick succession, that he could hardly count them. He had seen some of them die, – and had joked too, because they died with prayers upon their lips. With what a rattling noise the drop went down; and how suddenly they changed, from strong and vigorous men to dangling heaps of clothes!

Some of them might have inhabited that very cell – sat upon that very spot. It was very dark; why didn't they bring a light? The cell had been built for many years. Scores of men must have passed their last hours there. It was like sitting in a vault strewn with dead bodies – the cap, the noose, the pinioned arms, the faces that he knew, even beneath that hideous veil. – Light, light![7]

The devices here are simpler, but not ineffective. They help Dickens put over what was to him an experience of imaginative importance – as a journalist he had often visited and described the prisons of his time. We start with two 'times', the present (in which we read the text) and the past (in which the prisoner sits in his cell). The first small disturbance to this reassuring time-gap comes in the first paragraph, with *almost as it was delivered* : not 'almost as it *had been* delivered', referring to the further-

F

past of the court-room. The court-room scene is present in his mind, and this brings it closer to us than it would otherwise have been. The reminiscence of the judicial sentence follows this up with *that was the end*, though the interpretation is not clear : ' that had been the end (of what the judge had said) ' seems likely, but ' that was the end (of what he could remember) ' is possible. The point is in the confusion. The second paragraph returns us to the original tense-relationship with *he began to think* and reinforces it with the further-past of *had known* and *had died*. *They rose*, again, is to be expected since now he sees the dead before him as if they were in his cell. *He had seen* preserves the right tense-distances, and *had joked*, but *died* violates it : we should have *had died*. The moment of these past deaths is brought nearer to Fagin, and to the reader of course. And the re-enactment of the drop continues in the same tense but with the exclamatory forms lending themselves to dramatic immediacy nevertheless. It is in the last paragraph that all this pays off, especially if we remember Dicken's penchant for public readings, which were in the nature of dramatic events. First the further-past is re-established with *might have inhabited*. *Sat* avoids specifying the tense too closely, much would depend on intonation, and perhaps gesture if the hint of *that* is taken up dramatically. *It was very dark* repeats the visual impression at the opening of paragraph 2 and employs the right past tense for the cell. The interrogative, however, is in a form which suggests direct speech rather forcibly : not ' He wondered why *they didn't* bring a light ' but ' He wondered, " Why *don't they* bring a light?" ', with the question-intonation. The recurrence of a vivid visual impression of bodies in the cell (again making use of an ambiguous demonstrative, *that hideous veil*) brings, at last, the burst of direct speech and therefore also of the past into the (reading) present: *Light, light*! This cry relates, by contrast, with the pervading sense of darkness, so that syntax and symbolism work together at the point where the passage reaches its crisis. The devices are simple enough, and yet delicate enough too to be easily destroyed in translation or missed in a critical appraisal, especially the way in which Dickens lays the groundwork for tense-deviation early on in the passage. It seems worth considering a more complex use of similar features in a poem, Yeats's *Coole Park and Ballylee*.[8] The first verse depicts, in the present tense, the writer's house :

> Under my window-ledge the waters race . . .

It traces the course of the water as far as Coole demesne, where it spreads to a lake and drops underground.

> What's water but the generated soul?

The second verse runs as follows.

> Upon the border of that lake's a wood
> Now all dry sticks under a wintry sun,
> And in a copse of beeches there I stood,
> For Nature's pulled her tragic buskin on
> And all the rant's a mirror of my mood :
> At sudden thunder of the mounting swan
> I turned about and looked where branches break
> The glittering reaches of the flooded lake.

The present tense merges, as is normal, into the past tense in line 3, with *stood*, but changes back, abnormally, to the present, with *Nature's* and *rant's*, for Yeats is describing the past scene. He acknowledges this with *turned* and *looked* but switches to the present again with *break* (the lake was certainly flooded ' then ' – not necessarily ' now ', though it may be). The opening of verse 3 confirms this.

> Another emblem there ! That stormy white . . .

There and *that*, and the exclamatory form of the first phrase, indicate presence in the situation : but the situation we are ' present ' in, with Yeats, is of course the past one, in which he stood by the lake. The verse continues in the present tense, though the reference is to a state of affairs rather than a particular point in time, and verse 4 very skilfully avoids tense altogether :

> Sound of a stick upon the floor . . .

and continues without tense to the end. Only with verse 5 does tense return, this time the past tense :

> A spot whereon the founders lived and died
> Seemed once more dear than life . . .

And the present:

> We shift about – all that great glory spent –
> Like some poor arab tribesman and his tent.

So that the relationship of the present to the past is re-established
by the poem's end. What Yeats has done is confuse our sense of
time so that his 'composition of place' (the poem being a medita-
tion) can be the more vivid, bringing Coole before our eyes in
the present, only to snatch it back into the past and make us
feel the loss the more keenly. And this applies whether we accept
Yeats' view or not (I do not): he has put his feelings in such
a way as to enlist in his favour the tense-structure of English. It
is on occasions like this that stylistics can help the critic distinguish, if need be, the handling of language from general ideas,
and evaluate the two according to appropriate, and distinct,
criteria.[9]

In poetry, words and phrases can be related to each other by
the use of rhyme, by parallel placing in the line, and by other
devices not available to prose. But prose can employ other means
to achieve similar results, as we can see from Virginia Woolf's
handling of syntax and lexis in *To The Lighthouse* and *The
Waves*. The passages I have chosen deploy comparable structures and show, incidentally, how a writer may develop individual
techniques that suit his or her world-view. Virginia Woolf often
writes as if a single force were sometimes capable of blending
the disparate elements of existence into a whole. This impression
appears to have had particular significance for her. In *To The
Lighthouse*, the painter is engaged in manipulating reality
through her art so as to bring about such an effect, and her
activity seems to lie at the centre of the novel's meaning, not only
explicitly but implicitly too, since the novelist is engaged in a
similar task. The first passage is taken from the central section
of the novel, 'Time Passes', where the empty house is described
succumbing to time and the encroachment of the elements.

> Nothing it seemed could break that image, corrupt that
> innocence, or disturb the swaying mantle of silence which,
> week after week, in the empty room, wove into itself the fall-
> ing cries of birds, ships hooting, the drone and hum of the
> fields, a dog's bark, a man's shout, and folded them round
> the house in silence.[10]

This is only a short piece and is followed by long chains of repetitive syntax which the reader may find it interesting to look at for himself. But here there is more than syntactical repetition, though we shall start with that. Clearly, there are syntactical parallels that bring certain elements into semantic relationship:

break . . .	that image . . .
corrupt . . .	that innocence . . .
disturb . . .	the swaying mantle of silence . . .

The verbs are least interesting, since they are so closely related by meaning even without the help of syntax. But the relationship of *image, innocence* and *swaying mantle of silence* would prove worth elaborating in terms of the novel's central themes and associative connections, though that is beyond my present scope. The objects that follow *wove* can best be seen as parallel if their syntactical structure is transformed so as to eliminate what amounts almost to syntactical ' free variation ':

the falling *cries* . . .	of *birds* . . .
the *hooting* . . .	of *ships* . .
the *drone* and *hum* . . .	of the *fields* . .
the *bark* . . .	of a *dog* . . .
the *shout* . . .	of a *man* . . .

In this form, we see more clearly perhaps that each item involves *sounds*: *cries, hooting, drone, hum, bark, shout.* The actors are, indifferently, animal, inanimate, vegetable, human, and seem to have been chosen for their heterogeneity. The sounds of all these various outside disturbances are blended into one thing, their opposite: *silence.* And when we look again at the sentence as a whole, we see that its structure insists on this to the point of illogicality, but neatly pursuing the *mantle* metaphor:

Nothing it seemed could break that image, corrupt that innocence, or disturb *the swaying mantle of silence which* . . . *wove (the sounds)* . . . and *folded them* round the house *in silence.*

I have italicised the features that are of particular interest. They scarcely require comment, except perhaps to point out the way in which the sounds themselves form the mantle of silence, since it is woven of them, and that it is they that are *folded* round the house *in silence*, so assimilating the opposites completely to one predominant 'image', or 'innocence', that of the peculiar silence of a deserted house. This short passage shows skilful control of sentential meaning in terms of an underlying metaphor and submerged syntactical-lexical relationships. The same control emerges in the passage from *The Waves*.

> The sun struck straight upon the house, making the white walls glare between the dark windows. Their panes, woven thickly with green branches, held circles of impenetrable darkness. Sharp-edged wedges of light lay upon the window sill and showed inside the room plates with blue rings, cups with curved handles, the bulge of a great bowl, the criss-cross pattern in the rug and the formidable corners and lines of cabinets and bookcases. Behind their conglomeration hung a zone of shadow in which might be a further shape to be discovered or still denser depths of darkness.[11]

Here, the agent is light, and the subjects of each sentence reflect this :

> The sun . . .
> Their panes . . .
> Sharp-edged wedges of light . . .
> A zone of shadow . . .

The last, as befits its change of emphasis, is not placed at the head of the sentence but after (' behind ') *Behind their conglomeration*, (which refers to the features that *can* be seen). Emphasising the opposition of sun and shadow, the passage begins with *The sun struck straight upon the house, making the white walls glare between the dark windows*, and this opposition carries through the passage until we reach the emphasis on darkness at the end, *still denser depths of darkness*. The operation of light is again emphasised by the way in which objects behind the panes are described, predominantly in terms of geometrical shape – that is, in terms of light striking their surfaces or colours : *circles, rings, curved, bulge, criss-cross, pattern, corners, lines* and *shape* itself. Again, then, we have opposites unified, this time by being seen as the manifestation of one force, light, the unidirectional visual perspective being emphasised by the description of the room's contents. And again, a few transformations will clarify the point.

plates . . .	with blue *rings* . . .
cups . . .	with curved *handles* . . .
a great *bowl* . . .	with a *bulge* . . .
the *rug* . . .	with the *criss-cross pattern* . . .
the *cabinets* and *bookcases* . . .	with formidable *corners* and *lines* . . .

The technique is similar, though not identical, to that in the previous passage. The heterogeneous is again unified, the varied forms of domestic objects by their geometrical description and syntactical alliance, the sun and shadow by their relationship to light and the single direction of that light. The reader will have noticed that alliteration and other sound-effects have an important role to play in emphasising and relating the opposing forces : *sun struck straight / denser depths of darkness*, each with triple word-initial alliteration, and also in unifying certain phrases elsewhere, in obvious cases such as *sharp-edged wedges, bulge of a great bowl* or *corners and lines of cabinets and bookcases*, and more subtly throughout the four sentences. *Wove* and *folded* in the previous passage were vowel-linked, but the effect was less fully developed. When employed to this extent, it bears comparison even with extravagant poetic usage, such as that in Gerard Manley Hopkins' *God's Grandeur* : [12]

And all is seared with trade; bleared, smeared with toil;
And wears man's smudge, and shares man's smell . . .

where syntactic-auditory-semantic groupings are set up :

s*eared* . . .	with *t*rade . . .
bl*eared* . . .	} with *t*oil . . .
sm*eared* . . .	

w*ears* . . .	man's *sm*udge . . .
sh*ares* . . .	man's *sm*ell . . .

Patterning such as this (whether in verse or prose) is, of course, scarcely to be missed. The degree of repetition in the second Conrad passage or in these sentences of Virginia Woolf's is recognisable as unusual for speech, though it breaks no rules of the language. Again, the use of sound in the passage from *The Waves* goes beyond the occasional echoes that are found in many everyday sentences both by its density and by its organisation in relation to syntax and meaning. More typical of prose, and often going unrecognised in what we are accustomed to call poetry, is a mode of organisation that depends for its effect entirely on appropriateness to meaning, much as the *mask*-sentence from *The Secret Agent* did. Here is a simple example, from Malcolm Lowry's *Under the Volcano*, in which it cannot be said that there is deviation despite the relative complexity of the sentence.

> His passion for Yvonne (whether or not she'd ever been much good as an actress was beside the point, he'd told her the truth when he said she would have been more than good in any film he made) had brought back to his heart, in a way he could not have explained, the first time that alone, walking over the meadows from Saint Près, the sleepy French village of backwaters and locks and grey disused watermills where he was lodging, he had seen, rising slowly and wonderfully and with boundless beauty above the stubble fields blowing with wild flowers, slowly rising in the sunlight, as centuries before the pilgrims straying over those same fields had watched them rise, the twin spires of Chartres Cathedral.[13]

The elaboration of the basic sentence 'His passion . . . brought back . . . the first time that . . . he had seen . . . the twin spires of Chartres Cathedral' arrests the resolution of the syntax, and then releases it so as to coincide with the discovery of the twin spires, thus miming the consul's experience when discovering the cathedral and also, by analogy, his discovery of love, of his twinned relationship with his wife. Related images recur throughout the novel – principally the two volcanoes and the split rock, but also other images that are more reflections of doom than of relationship, especially that of the ravine into which, eventually, the consul's body is thrown, his death almost coinciding with Yvonne's as she tries to reach him through the forest. The introduction of the twin spires here, then, and the emphasis they receive, is of importance, and the sensitive reader will respond to Lowry's syntax so as to pick up the clue. How different the effect would have been if the sentence had run 'The first time he had seen the twin spires of Chartres Cathedral was brought back by his passion for Yvonne.' It is perhaps from such unspectacular uses of language that the young writer can learn most.

Another passage from the same novel illustrates the use that can be made of narrative convention, by deviating from it. The reader may like to write various versions of the following passage, changing it for example into the first person or preserving intact the third-person narrative mode in which it begins.

> He was sweating now, terribly; it was suddenly as hot in this little niche as in a telephone booth in New York during a heat wave; his hands trembled frantically; 66, Cafeasperina; Guzmán. Erikson 34. He had the number, had forgotten it: the name Zuzugoitea, Zuzugoitea, then Sanabria, came starting out of the book at him: Erikson 35. Zuzogoitea. He'd already forgotten the number, forgotten the number, 34, 35, 666: he was turning back the leaves, a large drop of sweat splashed on the book – this time he saw Vigil's name. But he'd already taken the receiver off the hook, the receiver off the hook, off the hook, he held it the wrong way up, speaking, splashing into the earhole, the mouth-hole, he could not hear – could they hear? see? – the earhole as before: ' ¿ *Qué quieres?* Who do you want . . . God!' he shouted, hanging up. He would need a drink to do this. He ran for the staircase but half-way up, shuddering, in a frenzy, started down again; I brought the tray down. No, the drinks are still up there. He came on the mirador and drank down all the drinks in sight.[14]

The consul, an alcoholic, attempting to make a phone-call, finds himself unable to control his mind and actions. The first sign that the third-person narration is miming the fluctuations of the consul's attention comes with *He'd already forgotten the number, forgotten the number*, and this effect is intensified with *But he'd already taken the receiver off the hook, the receiver off the hook, off the hook*, and with *speaking, splashing into the earhole, the mouth-hole, he could not hear – could they hear? see? – the earhole as before*. Syntactical abnormality, in the overlapping of phrases, is followed up by elliptical phrases that are themselves normal but do not supply the semantic clues we are accustomed to: the consul in his confusion is speaking into the earhole and splashing (sweating) into the mouth-hole. *Earhole* and *mouth-hole* themselves suggest difficulty with language. *Could they hear*, though still third-person, has the syntax of direct speech. The point is the same as that made about the Dickens passage: we have, not 'He wondered whether *they could* hear', but 'He wondered "*Can* they hear?"' with the third-person form *could* replacing *can*; and, again, the question-intonation. Lowry might well have learned the technique from Dickens, with whom it is a favourite, though of course it is used by others. As Blake said, 'The Bad Artist Seems to copy a Great deal – The Good one Really does Copy a great deal.' The abnormal way in which the consul's mind is working is also brought out by his thought that he might be 'seen' through the telephone. We get the operator's question repeated, and his translation of it, and then the ambiguous exclamation 'God!' all introduced in the normal way as reported speech. But after a short passage of straight third-person narration, but for *this* (re-establishing the norm, as Dickens also does towards the end of the prison passage) we get direct speech, unintroduced: *I brought the tray down. No, the drinks are still up there.* The use of *I* and *No* and *there* all emphasise the directness, so that read aloud it would have its effect as well as on the page. These two sentences deepen the sense of disorientation both by what they tell us about the consul and by their abnormality in the third-person mode of narration. And this has been the technique throughout: to allow formal deviations to coincide with the depiction of the consul's incapacity, so disturbing us, as readers, at the point that will bear best on Lowry's description of disturbance in his character. Anyone who has tried rewriting the passage will have found how hard it is to reap similar rewards from consistent narration. To suggest that Lowry would have done better, if he wanted to make us feel the consul's situation 'from inside', to narrate it for example in the first person would be to misunderstand the potentialities of deviation, relevantly used.

One last short piece, developing essentially the same point: this time, a passage from William Faulkner's *The Sound and the Fury*. In this case, too, 'traits of style' have a special significance which makes it worthwhile to abandon the descriptive approach used for the other passages. Benjy, a mentally deficient man suffering because of the absence of his beloved sister Caddie, is watching a game of . . . well, what?

Through the fence, between the curling flower spaces, I could see them hitting. They were coming towards where the flag was and I went along the fence. Luster was hunting in the grass by the flower tree. They took the flag out, and they were hitting. Then they put the flag back and they went to

the table, and he hit and the other hit. Then they went on,
and I went along the fence. Luster came away from the flower
tree and we went along the fence and they stopped and we
stopped and I looked through the fence while Luster was
hunting in the grass.

'Here, caddie.' He hit. They went across the pasture. I
held to the fence and watched them going away.

'Listen at you, now,' Luster said. 'Ain't you something,
thirty-three years old, going on that way. After I done went
all the way to town to buy you that cake. Hush up that moan-
ing. Ain't you going to help me find that quarter so I can go
to the show tonight.'

They were hitting little, across the pasture. I went back
along the fence to where the flag was. It flapped on the bright
grass and trees.[15]

Of course, the game is golf. Indirectly, we discover that Benjy
is weeping because the call of 'caddie' makes him think his sister
is somewhere at hand. And the reader understands, too, Luster's
self-centred insensitivity to Benjy's emotional situation. However, the true inwardness of Benjy's feelings is conveyed simply
by the language he uses, which shows us the limitation of his
mental horizon and thus, in the wider context of the story, the
desperateness of his need for Caddie, who alone loves him and
modifies her behaviour to take account of his affection and
limited understanding (so, for example, she washes off the scent
given her by her lover because it upsets and disorients Benjy).
The cumulative effect of Benjy's language is essential to its full
effect, and Faulkner gives us the whole opening section of the
novel in it, casting over events (later re-told by others) the primary
emotional interpretation given them by Benjy. This is therefore
a very thorough-going example of an author miming the thought
of his character, more thorough-going than Golding's in *The
Inheritors* since there is a greater distinction between the way
Benjy thinks and the 'normal' way than there is between
Neanderthal man's thought and ours, as Golding sees it: that is,
in fact, the pathos of Golding's presentation. As this passage
allows us to see them, what are the features of Benjy's language?
Hitting is always used here without an object, although the rules
of the language require one (here, *the ball* or *it*): this suggests a
poor grasp of causality, which is confirmed elsewhere (notably
when Benjy burns his hand). Benjy uses *went* rather than *walked*

or *moved*: *went* is a less normal choice in most of its appearances than one of the other words would have been (though it occurs normally in *they went on*) suggesting that Benjy fails to make certain semantic discriminations. Again, he uses descriptive phrases where most speakers would use a ready-made label: *curling flower spaces, where the flag was* (the 'green'), *the flower tree*. The same circumlocutions are resorted to by normal speakers when they attempt to describe unfamiliar objects, for which experts may have labels: Faulkner has observed and used one of the ways in which language normally works in order to give us insight into abnormality. Benjy predominantly uses the simplest linker, *and*, suggesting a certain difficulty in handling complex interrelationships, syntactical and other (the latter we gather also from the passage in general, especially from the analytic, linear way it develops instead of providing a synthetic statement of the situation). Minor features, like *hitting little* and *flapped on*, provide unsettling touches, again suggesting linguistic and mental limitations, a tendency to use simple categorisations in a childlike way. The reader will find other passages in the same novel, in the first and in the other sections, which deviate further from normal language or are in other respects of considerable interest.

Having seen a few of the ways in which prose can be organised, within short sections, so as to exploit linguistic and conventional possibilities, let us look now at a complete story, *The Blind Man*, which is printed in its entirety on pages 112–29 below.

I have chosen a story by Lawrence in order to make it easy for the reader to compare a writer's technique in prose with the same writer's technique in poetry (in this case in *The Blind Man* and *Gloire de Dijon* respectively). There is clearly an interesting area here for structural analysis. This particular story does, however, also illustrate very well the way in which overall narrative structure (what one might call macro-structure) may be reinforced, even influenced, by minor linguistic details (or micro-structure), and that is the main point I want to make about the value of stylistic analysis in dealing with the dominant structure even of larger prose works.[16]

The narrative structure of *The Blind Man* is largely made up of the movements of the three main characters, Maurice Pervin, his wife Isabel and her friend, Bertie Reid, who comes to visit the couple on their farm. The narration is in the third person, past tense. We first see Isabel waiting in the house for the two men to arrive from outside. Restless, she decides to fetch her husband from the stables. She finds him, brings him back to the house and, while he is upstairs cleaning up, welcomes Bertie on his arrival from the station. All three have dinner, but Maurice is slightly uneasy and leaves them in order to do some odd jobs in the stables, while Isabel and Bertie talk. This time, it is Bertie who goes out to fetch Maurice, finds him and brings him back to Isabel, who is waiting for them both in the house. Figure 4 summarises this.

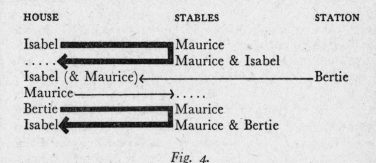

Fig. 4.

The journeys narrated in detail are those of Isabel and of Bertie to fetch Maurice from the stables, and they thus acquire perceptual prominence (represented in the diagram by the heavier line). It is also during the course of these two journeys that the principal psychological events take place, revealing the subject-matter of the story. Maurice himself goes out to the stables with positive relief, despite the foul weather and the darkness. He feels at home in the dark, being blind, but also because he has an affinity for *the animal grossness of the back*, his mind is slow but his emotions quick, his limbs *seemed to know the earth*. Maurice goes out alone, and willingly, whereas both Isabel and Bertie are *unwilling* and only go out to fetch him (as if they cannot accept his affinity with darkness). Isabel's journey serves an expository function, demonstrating to us the relationship of Isabel to her husband and to the forces he represents (p. 116ff). The second contains the denouement of the story, the crumbling of Bertie's personality in contact with Maurice (p. 126ff). There are echoes between the two journeys, for example a similar framework of references:

Isabel (p. 117)	*Bertie* (p. 126)
She pulled on her over-shoes, wrapped a large tartan shawl around her, put on a man's felt hat . . .	Bertie put on an old overcoat . . .
. . . and ventured out . . .	He went out . . .
She wished she had brought a lantern . . .	. . . and took a lantern . . .
Rain blew against her . . .	He shrank from the wet . . .
Half she liked it, half she felt unwilling to battle . . .	Unwilling, he went through it all . . .

Both wrap up, but Bertie takes a lantern whereas Isabel only wishes she had; both take the weather as an attack upon them (*against*, *shrank from*), but Isabel half-likes it whereas Bertie's unwillingness is total.[17] Isabel is less deeply at risk than Bertie; she has her accepted sexual contact with Maurice, and is bearing his child, while Bertie totally avoids sexual contacts, indeed any form of closeness, physical or psychological.[18] Maurice is in this sense almost literally the psychological touchstone for them both. To his wife, despite her fear, he is ultimately a source of strength: *he was a tower of darkness to her*,[19] that is, a 'tower of strength' in and through darkness. Darkness (he is 'a dark man', idiomatically: a blind man) symbolises the creative forces, essential to life and to all human sexual and psychological strength but destructive to the weak and fearful. In Bertie's case, Maurice's touch is destructive. Although there are no overt homosexual implications in this story, there are certainly sexual implications in the way Maurice's actions are described,[20] especially in the phrase *he seemed to take him* (Bertie) *in the soft travelling grasp*.[21] To Bertie, Maurice's touch reveals a terrible emptiness, *he was like a mollusc whose shell is broken* because *he had been touched by the blind man, his insane reserve broken in* (p. 129). Although Isabel, comparably, sometimes struggles 'to maintain her calm, composed, friendly bearing, *a sort of mask she wore all over her body*' (my italics),[22] still her body is also full with Maurice's child and that, with all its sexual and symbolic implications, makes all the difference. It is interesting to see that Lawrence also brings the two journeys together by the way in which he depicts Maurice's reactions. When he comes back with his wife to the house, *he stood at the foot of the stairs, arrested, listening . . . He seemed to be listening to fate* (p. 119). Immediately following this sentence, we have Maurice saying *He's not here yet*: clearly, it was Bertie he was listening for, even if he was listening ' to ' fate. And this interpretation is confirmed when he returns with Bertie to the house and the two men stand before Isabel: *Maurice stood with head uplifted, as if listening . . . He seemed to be listening to hear if it were real* (' it ' being *the fulfilment of mortal friendship* with Bertie) (p. 129). The fatal irony is complete. The two opposites, Maurice and Bertie, cannot understand or safely touch each other, only Isabel can understand and in some sense, in different senses, touch both.

On one hand, then, Isabel stands between the two men. On the other, Maurice is the focal point. These two ways of seeing the triadic relationship are worth exploring in a little more detail. The first might be delineated as follows:

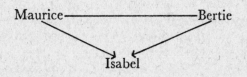

Maurice is English, passionate, very sensitive, a big man with powerful legs and strong provincial blood, mentally low. He is just the opposite of Bertie, who is Scotch, neuter, with emotions not so very fine, a small man with little short legs, and a quick, ironical mind (e.g., p. 114). Maurice is blind, Bertie's eyes are remarkable, showing an almost childlike intuition. The opposition is drawn in terms of parallel features (the list could be expanded). Isabel is Scotch and shares Bertie's intellectuality – she reviews for a Scottish newspaper – but she also cultivates an interest in agriculture and cattle-raising, while Maurice shares her literary activities and talks, sings and reads with her (p. 115). The farm emblematically illustrates the division and unity of man and wife – *the animal grossness of the back*, where Maurice is most at home, is complemented by *the handsome rooms in front*, which are *his*

wife's surroundings and have *a delicate, refined scent, very faintly
spicy*. He wavers and moves cautiously when he enters the house,
and yet these are *their own regions of repose and beauty* : there is
still a notion of shared, overlapping domains (p. 119). On the other
hand, when we take Maurice as the touchstone for the other
two, we get a different psychological pattern, which has already
been more fully explored because it receives such emphasis from
the narrative structure :

But it is the first pattern that receives emphasis at the opening
of the story, and it is this we must now take into account if we
are to grasp the structure of the story fully. Here is the complete
opening paragraph (p. 112).

> Isabel Pervin was listening for two sounds – for the sound of
> wheels on the drive outside and for the noise of her husband's
> footsteps in the hall. Her dearest and oldest friend, a man
> who seemed almost indispensable to her living, would drive
> up in the rainy dusk of the closing November day. The trap
> had gone to fetch him from the station. And her husband,
> who had been blinded in Flanders, and who had a disfiguring
> mark on his brow, would be coming in from the outhouses.

Ready as we are at this point to pick up every clue to the
characters, we must I think go on from this paragraph with a
certain predisposition to suppose that Isabel favours Bertie over
her husband. Of course, we discover almost immediately, too,
how deep her marital relationship goes, and yet we know that the
strains it has to bear are considerable, and that Bertie's visit may
provide some kind of relief, even escape. The opening paragraph
certainly places Isabel in the focal position, and Lawrence
enforces this point of view by the way he manipulates detail so
as to relate the two arrivals to each other (the journeys of
Maurice and of Bertie towards Isabel, a faint pre-figuration of
the later journeys towards Maurice when it is *Maurice* who does
the ' listening '). Let us look at this more closely. It shows a

similar device to Conrad's in the murder passage, used for a
different purpose, which reminds us of the importance of taking
function into account in discussing technique.[23]

Isabel Pervin was listening for two sounds –
1 for the sound . . .   of wheels . . .
2 and for the noise . . .   of her husband's footsteps . . .

1 on the drive outside . . .
2 in the hall . . .

1 Her dearest and oldest friend, a man . . .
2 and her husband . . .

1 who seemed almost indispensable . . .
2 who had been blinded . . . and who had a disfiguring mark . . .

1 to her living . . .   would drive . . .   up . . .
2 in Flanders . . . on   would be coming   in . . .
   his brow . . .

1 in the rainy dusk of the closing November day.
2 from the outhouses . . .

Only one sentence, *The trap had gone to fetch him from the
station*, stands outside this syntactic-semantic parallelism. Isabel
listens for *two sounds*, and from this point onward, the two men
are described so as to be seen in *relation to* each other and *moving
towards* Isabel, a narrative parallel to the psychological situation :

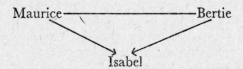

Or rather, a potential narrative parallel, since these journeys
never take place as foreseen here, and are only echoed at the
end when Maurice and Bertie do come in from outside to a
waiting Isabel, but come together :

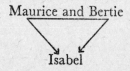

On this occasion, Isabel first *hears* the two men coming, *Isabel, as they came, thought their footsteps sounded strange* (p. 129), which serves to remind us of the opening paragraph. This fulfilment of the pattern, in an unexpected form, reinforces the ironic fulfilment of *Maurice's* 'listening'. Isabel's listening, too, has an unexpected outcome, since she sees her friend Bertie destroyed and has been forced to acknowledge, partially against her will, the depth of her contact with her husband, disfigured, frightening and partly misled though he may be. By contrast, Bertie, after all, is not *indispensable to her living*, he only *seemed* so (Lawrence's use of the word is ubiquitous! – but here it is appropriate). If we look again at the narrative outline of the story, adding these potential journeys (Figure 5), an interesting structure emerges which is, I think, fully operative perceptually.

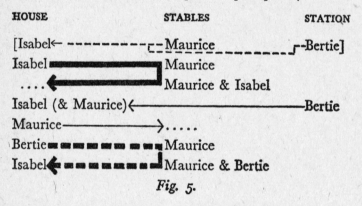

Fig. 5.

The story has what might be called a dual perspective. That which occupies the body of the narration places Maurice at the focal point. That which the opening paragraph leads us to expect recurs only at the end, in an altered form, but coinciding with the final movement of the first perspective. The beauty of the structure is, of course, that the two perspectives not only, by the end, coincide structurally, but also reinforce each other thematically. This is perhaps a case of that ambiguity of structure mentioned in the introduction. For the point of *The Blind Man* is only partly that two different people, Isabel and Bertie, react differently to certain forces and fears. This serves to illustrate the nature of the forces involved. But ultimately more important still is the *sexual relevance* of these reactions. Therefore it is finally the woman's view of the two men that must dominate the story. She must see them, not as she does at the beginning, but as she does at the end, however bitter the knowledge may be. And this is what the emergence of the hidden perspective achieves.[24]

Aspects of the story such as the lexical repetitions and lexical sets Lawrence employs have by no means been fully explored. The reader may care to complete the analysis of these and relate his findings to the same features as they operate not only in *Gloire de Dijon* but also in other stories by Lawrence, such as *The Horse Dealer's Daughter* (especially, in the latter, the lexis of the graveyard, pond and love-making scenes). Again, the structural significance for example of the passage describing Maurice alone upstairs (represented in round brackets in the plan) would bear investigation : in it, we glimpse the nature of Maurice's fears and their opposition to the fears of Isabel and Bertie.[25] But my purpose here has been to draw a general outline rather than a detailed picture, concentrating on types of inter-relationship that are too often ignored in the exploration of prose.

Chapter V

The type of structure we have been for the most part exploring, in verse and prose, does not occur throughout every work or in all good writing, as the reader will realise, but it does occur much more frequently than seems to have been recognised, particularly at points of intense communication, where not only the general impression given by the language but also the minutest fluctuations of the reader's response need to be controlled. Many of the passages I have selected for discussion involve the reader dramatically by creating, in formal terms, effects analogous to those being described at the level of meaning: bluntly put, the 'lurching' internal syntax of *Flying Crooked*, the 'concentration' of lexical and auditory activity in verse 2 of *Gloire de Dijon*, the 'folding' syntactical-lexical structure of the 'Time Passes' passage, the way Dickens brings Fagin closer to us as the past comes closer to Fagin, Lowry's disturbance of narrative convention as the consul struggles with the telephone, lexical and syntactical parallelisms in *The Blind Man*, and the rest. Mimesis of this kind is by no means the whole story, of course. Dominant structures tend to be made up, as we have seen, of subtle interactions many of which could not be called mimetic without stretching the term to the point of uselessness. And we must always remember that the same formal features, of sound, syntax, lexis, may be interpreted as miming different meanings, according to the overall semantic impact of the passage in which they appear.[1] This is something that has seldom been sufficiently well understood in relation to effects such as alliteration. The point is, again, the way human perception works, the tendency to interpret forms as meaningful within a given context. I hope that, although clearly there is further to go and more rigorously, I have been able to show at least that the direction is a fruitful one.

The relevance for criticism of looking at works as taking place in time, and building up through time a dominant structure, can be illustrated from yet one more angle, in some ways the most interesting. We have looked at a completed translation and at completed poems and prose passages, and at a short story. Let us look now at an incomplete work, and its completion, variant readings of Yeats' *Song of Wandering Aengus*.[2]

1	I went out to the hazel wood,	....
2	Because a fire was in my head,	....
3	And cut and peeled a hazel wand,	.... hazel rod
4	And hooked a berry to a thread;	And put a berry on a ...
5	And when white moths were on the wing,	....
6	And moth-like stars were flickering out,	And stars like moths were shining out
7	I dropped the berry in a stream	....
8	And caught a little silver trout.	And hooked a ....
9	When I had laid it on the floor	... had laid it on a stool
10	I went to blow the fire aflame,	I bent to ....
		I stooped to ....
11	But something rustled on the floor,	.... on the? stool
12	And some one called me by my name:	.... someone ....
13	It had become a glimmering girl	.... a laughing girl
14	With apple blossom in her hair	.... blossoms ....
15	Who called me by my name and ran	That called ....
16	And faded through the brightening air.	....
17	Though I am old with wandering	....
18	Through hollow lands and hilly lands,	In barren hills and marshy land
		Through hilly lands and hollow lands
19	I will find out where she has gone,	.... is gone
20	And kiss her lips and take her hands;	....
21	And walk among long dappled grass,	And walk and walk through summer grass

22 And pluck till time and times ....
    are done
23 The silver apples of the moon, ...
24 The golden apples of the sun. ....

The poem printed in full is the final version. On the right are variant readings, showing in two cases (lines 10 and 18) two earlier versions in chronological order. The reader has already seen Yeats's finished version of *Coole Park and Ballylee* and may find it interesting to follow the same poet's restructuring of this slighter poem, since even here it is evident that more than local effect is being taken into account during the course of composition. We can see the same mind at work that manipulated the tense-structure of *Coole Park and Ballylee*, aware of subtle and widely-spaced interconnections. The changes, as we shall see, make firmer certain tendencies, so that, by the end, the poem has a clear and relevant dominant structure. We can never say that more steps might not have been taken in the same direction, or different steps altogether. But we *can* say that the steps we trace through the variants result in a comparatively ' better ' *gestalt*, for the actual final version, than is evident in the first drafts. We shall be able to see this most clearly if we explore the final version and relate the others to it.

The second line of the poem suggests to us that the fishing is metaphorical, and the actual *fire* of verse 2 takes on metaphorical connotations as a result. The association of the fish with the fire in that verse (it rustles as the man goes to – Irish dialect for ' is about to ' – *blow the fire aflame*) anticipates and is prolonged through further associations of the fish with brightness : it is caught when *white moths* and *stars* are *flickering* (the word is related to both, to the moths that flicker on the wing and to the stars that vary their light); it is *silver* and becomes a *glimmering* girl with *apple-blossom* in her hair, who *fades* but only into the *brightening* of dawn, to be found again in a place of light where the grass is *dappled*. Metaphorically, she fades from the real world of night and day (day banishes her, as it does all spirits) but she will be found again in an idyllic world which is endless *till time and times are done*. He will enjoy with her the fruition of the promise made him by the *apple-blossom in her hair*, plucking in her company the fruit of both night and day :

      The silver apples of the moon,
      The golden apples of the sun.

The full chain of imagery related to light is established only in the final version. Let us look at each variant. There is one apparent loss, of *shining* in line 6. But considered more closely, *flickering* has the advantage, as we have seen, of conveying brightness as effectively in relation to the stars (probably more so, since attention is focused on variations of light), and adding an implication of brightness to the phrase *on the wing* that precedes it in a parallel position in the previous line: the two lines are so constructed as to bring out this association. In addition, the metaphorical implications render more finely the fitfulness of the vision that is to come. The substitution of *glimmering* for *laughing* eliminates the too robust impression given by the earlier choice, but more importantly provides the only unambiguous association of the girl herself with brightness, though of course the trout was *silver* and the blossom is white and is associated with silver, once we reach the end of the poem, through the *silver apples of the moon*, reflecting the girl's original association with night. *Dappled*, in line 21, similarly functions in two ways, replacing the inappropriate seasonal reference of *summer* (since we are in an idyllic setting) but nevertheless, and more forcibly, emphasising light, indifferently of *moon* or *sun* (perhaps we should understand that both are present simultaneously, but if not that each shines in turn so as to perpetually dapple the grass with light). All three changes, then, bear directly on the chain of light-imagery that seems central to the poem, and increases its stability and width of semantic implication.

The sense of fatedness running through the poem depends on this use of imagery but also on other features. Each of the protagonist's actions lead him towards one outcome and there are echoes almost too subtle to describe between verses 1 and 3, those in which he acts in reply to the ' fire ' in his head:

Verse 1

| I went out (to the . . . wood) | cut, peeled (a wand) | hooked, dropped (a/the berry) | caught (a . . . silver trout) |

Verse 3

| I will find out (where she has gone) | kiss, take (her lips, . . . hands) | walk (among . . . grass) | pluck (the silver apples . . ., the golden apples . . .) |

The echoes are fleeting enough, but the reader may agree that they function in his perception of the poem as in mine and are relevant to its thematic development, the first, second and fourth columns especially contributing to a sense of fulfilment at the close: the relation of the *wand* (replacing *rod* which has no magical connotations) to *her* eventual re-apparition is one of the most sensitive of these touches. The emphasis in verse 2 on *called me by my name*, which is twice repeated (lines 12 and 15), provides the impression of an urgent and personal call to which the protagonist must respond. And indeed we see that he has spent his life in response to it: the first two verses are in the past tense, he is now *old with wandering* and yet certain that his quest will reach its fated conclusion: *I will find out*. This confidence is supported by the inclusion of past, present and future in one synoptic vision of a life devoted to a single quest, as it is by the abolition of the unpleasant connotations of *barren* and *marshy* and finally the rearrangement of *hilly* and *hollow* so as to provide the traditional upward movement of a successful metaphorical journey:

> Though I am old with wandering
> Through hollow lands and hilly lands,
> I will find out where she has gone . . .

Again, the first verse runs rapidly through a series of actions, *I went . . . and cut and peeled . . . and hooked . . . and . . . I dropped . . . and caught*; the second, after the four lines recording the moment of apparition, moves forward rapidly in a different way, through a series of run-on lines, *girl/With apple-blossom in her hair/Who called me . . . and ran/And faded . . .* (the last run-on echoing the device of the first verse and so bringing to the fore an association between the man's impulse to fish, on one hand, and the girl's to flee on the other, his life of wandering being the inevitable outcome). Verse 3, though the search is not concluded in the present, seems to foreshadow it, by means of the subtle echoes we have already seen between verses 1 and 3, but also by picking up and intensifying parallelistic effects from earlier verses, so increasing the sense of stability as against that of forward movement: the two impulses are held in tension, awaiting the future.

V.1   When white moths were on the wing,

And moth-like stars were flickering out . . . .

V.2   When I had laid it on the floor . . .
        But something rustled on the floor . . . .

        But something rustled on the floor,
        And some one called me by my name.

        And some one called me by my name . . .
        Who called me by my name . . .

V.3   Through hollow lands and hilly lands . . .

        And kiss her lips and take her hands . . .

        And pluck till time and times are done . . .

        The silver apples of the moon,
        The golden apples of the sun.

As the reader will have noticed, parallelism of sound and meaning is increased in the last verse, and made to function several
times *within* the line-unit instead of only between lines. Much
of this structure was there from the start, but in verse 3 the
alterations become important, *hills . . . land* becoming *lands . . .
lands*, and the two adjectives developing parallelistic traits, *hilly
. . . hollow* (word-initial /h/, + central /l/ + vowel ending),
the semantic implications also being parallel (opposites). The
sense of stability given by this is helped by another feature that
comes about through two particularly sensitive alterations: that
of *in*, line 18, to *through*, and that of *through*, line 21, to *among*.
This emphasises that the protagonist ' passes through' the lands
of his search, but will 'stay among' the idyllic pastures *where
she has gone. Is gone*, again, changes to *has gone*, eliminating a
purposeless echo between *is gone* and *are done* (lines 19 and 22)
and also the hiatus /ʃɪ: ɪz/, but more importantly making her
absence seem less final: she 'is' not gone, she merely 'has'
gone and can be found. Again, *walk and walk* might convey a
sense of endless journeying and of weariness, just where the
opposite is needed. The new line avoids this and adds the
implications of *long* as well as *dappled*, *long* serving as a subtle
substitute for *summer* without dragging in the unwanted seasonal
reference.

Elements of structure which relate to the association of the
girl with brightness, the fatedness of the journey and the fore-

seen stability and perfection of its outcome are all made firmer
by the alterations Yeats makes, minor as most of these at first
appear. The reader will see that others, not mentioned here, also
have a role to play in perfecting the poem. But those which I
have considered show best the structural direction of Yeats's
creative effort. How easily such delicate touches might be lost
by a translator, as were Valéry's! So much depends on linguistic
features whose effects are seen not in isolation but only in relation
to the whole.

Before briefly considering certain issues related to evaluation, I
want to say something about what has not been covered by this
book, and about the uncertainty of what has been said on how
dominant structures are built up perceptually.

The reader may well be aware of the excellent work that has
already been done in stylistics on traits of style in individual
authors or in periods of literature. This kind of work should be
greatly expanded and carried out with more of an eye to the
function and interrelationship of elements and structures described. Clearly, such work must bear on the analysis of dominant
structures, since the perceptual effects of language in a given
work always depend partly, sometimes entirely, on the background of perception outside the work.[3] This will already be
obvious, but here is one more example, of a kind we have not
yet seen, provided by Henry Reed's *Judging Distances*, which first
uses arms-practice lingo and then poeticalese only to blend the
first with genuinely poetic perception into a witty and meaningful
new language at the close :

> There may be dead ground in between; and I may not have got
> The knack of judging a distance; I will only venture
> A guess that perhaps between me and the apparent lovers,
> (Who, incidentally, appear by now to have finished)
> At seven o'clock from the houses, is roughly a distance
> Of about one year and a half.

The reader who knows this poem will agree that no adequate
study of its structure could be made without reference to a
description of the linguistic backgrounds to which it appeals and
of the significance of the new language Reed has created, by-
passing both.[4]

Another function of stylistics might be to help us uncover with some precision effects analogous to quotation in music. Here is an example from Keats's *Ode to a Nightingale*, from the opening two lines.

> My heart aches, and a drousy numbness pains
> My sense. . . .

This *Ode* is of course concerned with the desire for voluntary death and the fear of what that might entail. There is a thematic similarity between Keats's poem and Hamlet's famous soliloquy, *To be or not to be*, though Hamlet fears not what he may miss in this life but what may come to him in the next. The contrast is only partial, though, since the *Ode* begins with the wish to escape old age and only later turns to the delights of being alive. But there are more than thematic echoes involved, as the following parallelism indicates:

K: My heart aches, and a   drousy   numbness pains
S: The heart ache, and the thousand natural   shocks

K: My sense. . . .[5]
S: That flesh is heir to. . . .[6]

The way all the words relate to the stress-pattern of the line is the same, assuming Shakespeare's line is decasyllabic. Up to the caesura, which comes after the third syllable in both lines, we have identical lexical items *heart* and *ache*. *And* follows the caesura in both, then two determiners, *a* and *the*, then an adjective in each, the sounds of which are similar, / ɑʊ / and /θ/ appearing in both, the initial /d/ being related to /o/ phonetically, so that we have the parallel sequences

$$/d \ldots \text{ɑʊ} \ldots z/$$
$$/θ \ldots \text{ɑʊ} \ldots z/$$

Numbness and *natural* again fall into the same position in the line and are phonetically related, /n . . . ə . . ./ appearing in each in comparable positions. *Pains* and *shocks* fall into the same line-position before a run-on and are related semantically, as are *sense* and *flesh* on the following line, with the addition of the repetition of /e/. Moreover, the Shakespearean echo on /k/ between *ache* and *shocks* is paralleled by the echo on /ei/ in Keats's line, between the comparable items *aches* and *pains*, in both cases the sound-link underlining a semantic link. To summarise the dominant traits of the parallelism: the word-stress relationship is identical, the caesura comes at the same place, there is a run-on in both, all the lexical items are related to each other by sense, sound or both, and the grammatical items are mostly related too, even though the overall grammatical structure of the phrases is different. Conscious or not, such similarities amount to a reference to the Hamlet soliloquy at the beginning of Keats's *Ode*. Not to take account of this opening reference, and the hint it offers as to the theme of the *Ode*, would be to fail in catching an aspect of the poem that bears on our perception of its dominant structure throughout.[7]

So much for types of analysis that have not been undertaken. And much could be added.[8] With regard, however, to the study of dominant structures, which have been the focus of attention, I should like to avoid any summary that might give the impression that there is (or might one day be) some predetermined analytical 'sieve' through which a literary work could be passed so as to leave the critic with the dominant structure or structures.[9] The explorations I have undertaken show, I think, that every work must be treated as unique, with its own balance of formal-semantic interactions and pressures. As a 'rule of thumb' we can remember that linguistic patterning may be brought out analytically by looking, as I have said, *along* each rank within the levels of syntax or phonology[10] (Figure 6); or we may look *across* ranks, and levels, so as to pick up co-incidences (Figure 7).

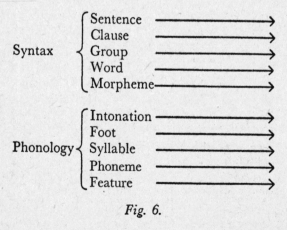

Fig. 6.

But we must remember that what we pick up analytically has still to be understood as part of a perceptual whole: its mere *presence* does not tell us what its *importance* may be. And there may be syntactical and phonological aspects that will not show up on such a simple ' grid '.

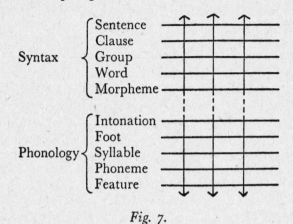

Fig. 7.

Lexical features – lexical sets, lexical repetition, co-occurrences, syntactical positioning and so on – have also to be taken into account. And we must relate events at all levels with each other and with formal poetic (and other) structures, and to wider aspects of meaning.[11] Deviation, as we have seen, has a complex role, bringing into play backgrounds of *langue*, *parole* (speech-expectations, but also ' register ', social, geographical, etc.), literary language and the work itself.[12] And finally, there is the mere semantic appropriateness of form, which cannot be detected in terms of unusual frequency, of patterning or of deviation, but only by a sensitive openness to linguistic significance in the most informal sense.[13]

It is evident that since the intrinsic and relative prominence of given linguistic features within different given works, and their frequency, is infinitely variable – and they may be combined in an infinite variety of ways both with each other and with meanings – we can only rely, ultimately, on the direct human perception of individual works.[14] This is no reason for not carrying conscious critical awareness as far as it will go. The point about the function of critical method in the total critical *response* is much the same as the point about the function of technical skill in verbal *creation*. The greater his skill, the more freely the writer is able to follow the direction of his creative impulse. But that

impulse itself, like the reader's response to its results, is something
that cannot be produced by following rules, only experienced as
a capacity of human living.

A number of comments have been made, in the practical chapters
and elsewhere, implying attitudes to evaluation which had better
be made as explicit, now, as the restricted aim of this book
allows.

We should distinguish, it seems to me, various kinds of evaluation, carried out according to various different criteria. The
critic has, at different times, to concern himself with the social
impact of literature, with its accuracy to historical or psychological ' reality ', with philosophical or aesthetic values as these
are expressed in, or bear on, verbal art. In assessing a work in
these quite distinct ways, the critic refers, or should refer, to
explicit criteria derived from those disciplines whose business
it is to evolve them. The notion of a single evaluative statement –
' this is a good/bad poem/story/novel ' – appears, when carefully considered, no better than preposterous. Indeed, a blanket
stylistic judgement would seem equally inadequate, any work
containing such a variety of features. But stylistic evaluation is,
at least, central to literary criticism, because it alone deals directly
with the use and perceptual effect of *language*. As we saw at the
beginning, this is what distinguishes literary criticism from any
other kind, from the criticism of film, music, painting, architecture,
each with its own medium, its own restraints and opportunities
and mode of impinging on our senses. And this is why, of course,
evaluative solutions such as I. A. Richards's, in *Principles of
Literary Criticism*, are unsatisfactory : they would apply equally
(if at all) to other arts.

Within the central stylistic area of critical evaluation – that
which, in the case of *Coole Park and Ballylee*, would concern
itself with the way Yeats puts over his theme linguistically, rather
than with its other aspects – the criteria we have to appeal to
are as yet by no means clear, possibly because they are derivable
partly from linguistics and partly from perceptual psychology.
(The same holds good, of course, of the criticism of any art :
both the medium and perceptual factors have to be taken into
account, though this does not always seem to be understood and
may therefore strike one as strange when brought out in relation
to verbal art.)

As regards one aspect of stylistic evaluation, however, a few more points can be made. I hope the reader will agree that they accord naturally enough with the practical work we have done. I have assumed that stylistics can accept as fundamental the linguist's insight into the semantic nature of language. Almost all linguistic elements that are perceived by speakers serve to distinguish meanings, or have meanings. *Utterances are responded to as carriers of meaning.* It would therefore seem unnatural, as I have already argued, to suppose that in the case of literature this all-pervasive attitude undergoes a change. We might more easily believe it to be intensified. And this is in fact what we observe when we consider our usual evaluative responses. However, we have I think to go further. If, in literature, form becomes a focus of semantic curiosity because of the way ' accidents ' are ' redeemed ' (as I also argued in an earlier chapter), we must accept that linguistic structuring may detract from, as well as be appropriate to, the communication of meaning. There can be no *merely* aesthetic effects. Any formal emphases, any linkages, will necessarily bear on meaning, and if they are not appropriate or are inappropriate to it they must distract the reader, however unconsciously, and will have to be positively discounted in his interpretation of the whole.[15] This is not only a waste of potentialities of the medium, but also an obstruction to the flow of communication and must be judged as such. Borderline cases are those in which the formal features involved are intrinsically weak enough to fade into insignificance if, like the nose/blot in the drawing, they fail to have a semantic function. And we must remember that, in any utterance, there is an infinity of minute cross-hatchings of formal relationship that normally and properly pass unnoticed.[16]

What we have been watching, in the language of verse and prose, is an extension of the means commonly exploited by language to control meanings. *Langue* consists of general patterns of form and meaning which guarantee the communicative value of any utterance whatever. However, the structure of individual, unique utterances may exploit form so as to make additional semantic use of material features such as sounds and sequential patterns that are not essential to *langue* and would not necessarily appear in the same message otherwise coded.[17] This represents a deeper saturation of form by meaning, beyond (as it were) the call of linguistic duty.[18] What we see on these occasions is how natural language works at full stretch in *parole*.

Appendix
The Blind Man

Isabel Pervin was listening for two sounds – for the sound of wheels on the drive outside and for the noise of her husband's footsteps in the hall. Her dearest and oldest friend, a man who seemed almost indispensable to her living, would drive up in the rainy dusk of the closing November day. The trap had gone to fetch him from the station. And her husband, who had been blinded in Flanders, and who had a disfiguring mark on his brow, would be coming in from the outhouses.

He had been home for a year now. He was totally blind. Yet they had been very happy. The Grange was Maurice's own place. The back was a farmstead, and the Wernhams, who occupied the rear premises, acted as farmers. Isabel lived with her husband in the handsome rooms in front. She and he had been almost entirely alone together since he was wounded. They talked and sang and read together in a wonderful and unspeakable intimacy. Then she reviewed books for a Scottish newspaper, carrying on her old interest, and he occupied himself a good deal with the farm. Sightless, he could still discuss everything with Wernham, and he could also do a good deal of work about the place – menial work, it is true, but it gave him satisfaction. He milked the cows, carried in the pails, turned the separator, attended to the pigs and horses. Life was still very full and strangely serene for the blind man, peaceful with the almost incomprehensible peace of immediate contact in darkness. With his wife he had a whole world, rich and real and invisible.

They were newly and remotely happy. He did not even regret the loss of his sight in these times of dark, palpable joy. A certain exultance swelled his soul.

But as time wore on, sometimes the rich glamour would leave them. Sometimes, after months of this intensity, a sense of burden overcame Isabel, a weariness, a terrible *ennui,* in that silent house approached between a colonnade of tall-shafted pines. Then she felt she would go mad, for she could not bear it. And sometimes he had devastating fits of depression, which seemed to lay waste his whole being. It was worse than depression – a black misery, when his own life was a torture to him, and when his presence was unbearable to his wife. The dread went down to the roots of her soul as these black days recurred. In a kind of panic she tried to wrap herself up still further in her husband. She forced the old spontaneous cheerfulness and joy to continue. But the effort it cost her was almost too much. She knew she could not keep it up. She felt she would scream with the strain, and would give anything, anything, to escape. She longed to possess her husband utterly; it gave her inordinate joy to have him entirely to herself. And yet, when again he was gone in a black and massive misery, she could not bear him, she could not bear herself; she wished she could be snatched away off the earth altogether, anything rather than live at this cost.

Dazed, she schemed for a way out. She invited friends, she tried to give him some further connexion with the outer world. But it was no good. After all their joy and suffering, after their dark, great year of blindness and solitude and unspeakable nearness, other people seemed to them both shallow, prattling, rather impertinent. Shallow prattle seemed presumptuous. He became impatient and irritated, she was wearied. And so they lapsed into their solitude again. For they preferred it.

But now, in a few weeks' time, her second baby would be born. The first had died, an infant, when her husband first went out to France. She looked with joy and relief to the coming of the second. It would be her salvation. But also she felt some anxiety. She was thirty years old, her husband was a year younger. They both wanted the child very much. Yet she could not help feeling afraid. She had her husband on her hands, a terrible joy to her, and a terrifying burden. The child would occupy her love and attention. And then, what of Maurice? What would he do? If only she could feel that he, too, would be at peace and happy when the child came! She did so want to luxuriate in a rich, physical satisfaction of maternity. But the man, what would he do? How could she provide for him, how avert those shattering black moods of his, which destroyed them both?

She sighed with fear. But at this time Bertie Reid wrote to Isabel. He was her old friend, a second or third cousin, a Scotch-

H

man, as she was a Scotchwoman. They had been brought up near to one another, and all her life he had been her friend, like a brother, but better than her own brothers. She loved him – though not in the marrying sense. There was a sort of kinship between them, an affinity. They understood one another instinctively. But Isabel would never have thought of marrying Bertie. It would have seemed like marrying in her own family.

Bertie was a barrister and a man of letters, a Scotchman of the intellectual type, quick, ironical, sentimental, and on his knees before the woman he adored but did not want to marry. Maurice Pervin was different. He came of a good old country family – the Grange was not a very great distance from Oxford. He was passionate, sensitive, perhaps over-sensitive, wincing – a big fellow with heavy limbs and a forehead that flushed painfully. For his mind was slow, as if drugged by the strong provincial blood that beat in his veins. He was very sensitive to his own mental slowness, his feelings being quick and acute. So that he was just the opposite to Bertie, whose mind was much quicker than his emotions, which were not so very fine.

From the first the two men did not like each other. Isabel felt that they *ought* to get on together. But they did not. She felt that if only each could have the clue to the other there would be such a rare understanding between them. It did not come off, however. Bertie adopted a slightly ironical attitude, very offensive to Maurice, who returned the Scotch irony with English resentment, a resentment which deepened sometimes into stupid hatred.

This was a little puzzling to Isabel. However, she accepted it in the course of things. Men were made freakish and unreasonable. Therefore, when Maurice was going out to France for the second time, she felt that, for her husband's sake, she must discontinue her friendship with Bertie. She wrote to the barrister to this effect. Bertram Reid simply replied that in this, as in all other matters, he must obey her wishes, if these were indeed her wishes.

For nearly two years nothing had passed between the two friends. Isabel rather gloried in the fact; she had no compunction. She had one great article of faith, which was, that husband and wife should be so important to one another, that the rest of the world simply did not count. She and Maurice were husband and wife. They loved one another. They would have children. Then let everybody and everything else fade into insignificance outside this connubial felicity. She professed herself quite happy and ready to receive Maurice's friends. She was happy and ready : the happy wife, the ready woman in possession. Without knowing why, the friends retired abashed and came no more. Maurice, of course, took as much satisfaction in this connubial absorption as Isabel did.

He shared in Isabel's literary activities, she cultivated a real interest in agriculture and cattle-raising. For she, being at heart perhaps an emotional enthusiast, always cultivated the practical side of life, and prided herself on her mastery of practical affairs. Thus the husband and wife had spent the five years of their married life. The last had been one of blindness and unspeakable intimacy. And now Isabel felt a great indifference coming over her, a sort of lethargy. She wanted to be allowed to bear her child in peace, to nod by the fire and drift vaguely, physically, from day to day. Maurice was like an ominous thunder-cloud. She had to keep waking up to remember him.

When a little note came from Bertie, asking if he were to put up a tombstone to their dead friendship, and speaking of the real pain he felt on account of her husband's loss of sight, she felt a pang, a fluttering agitation of re-awakening. And she read the letter to Maurice.

'Ask him to come down,' he said.

'Ask Bertie to come here!' she re-echoed.

'Yes – if he wants to.'

Isabel paused for a few moments.

'I know he wants to – he'd only be too glad,' she replied. 'But what about you, Maurice? How would you like it?'

'I should like it.'

'Well – in that case – But I thought you didn't care for him –'

'Oh, I don't know. I might think differently of him now,' the blind man replied. It was rather abstruse to Isabel.

'Well, dear,' she said, 'if you're quite sure –'

'I'm sure enough. Let him come,' said Maurice.

So Bertie was coming, coming this evening, in the November rain and darkness. Isabel was agitated, racked with her old restlessness and indecision. She had always suffered from this pain of doubt, just an agonising sense of uncertainty. It had begun to pass off, in the lethargy of maternity. Now it returned, and she resented it. She struggled as usual to maintain her calm, composed, friendly bearing, a sort of mask she wore over all her body.

A woman had lighted a tall lamp beside the table, and spread the cloth. The long dining-room was dim, with its elegant but rather severe pieces of old furniture. Only the round table glowed softly under the light. It had a rich, beautiful effect. The white cloth glistened and dropped its heavy, pointed lace corners almost to the carpet, the china was old and handsome, creamy-yellow, with a blotched pattern of harsh red and deep blue, the cups large and bell-shaped, the teapot gallant. Isabel looked at it with superficial appreciation.

Her nerves were hurting her. She looked automatically again at the high, uncurtained windows. In the last dusk she could just perceive outside a huge fir-tree swaying its boughs: it was as if she thought it rather than saw it. The rain came flying on the window panes. Ah, why had she no peace? These two men, why did they tear at her? Why did they not come – why was there this suspense?

She sat in a lassitude that was really suspense and irritation. Maurice, at least, might come in – there was nothing to keep him out. She rose to her feet. Catching sight of her reflection in a mirror, she glanced at herself with a slight smile of recognition, as if she were an old friend to herself. Her face was oval and calm, her nose a little arched. Her neck made a beautiful line down to her shoulder. With hair knotted loosely behind, she had something of a warm, maternal look. Thinking this of herself, she arched her eyebrows and her rather heavy eyelids, with a little flicker of a smile, and for a moment her grey eyes looked amused and wicked, a little sardonic out of her transfigured Madonna face.

Then, resuming her air of womanly patience – she was really fatally self-determined – she went with a little jerk towards the door. Her eyes were slightly reddened.

She passed down the wide hall, and through a door at the end. Then she was in the farm premises. The scent of dairy, and of farm-kitchen, and of farm-yard and of leather almost overcame her: but particularly the scent of dairy. They had been scalding out the pans. The flagged passage in front of her was dark, puddled and wet. Light came out from the open kitchen door. She went forward and stood in the doorway. The farm-people were at tea, seated at a little distance from her, round a long, narrow table, in the centre of which stood a white lamp. Ruddy faces, ruddy hands holding food, red mouths working, heads bent over the tea-cups: men, land-girls, boys: it was teatime, feeding-time. Some faces caught sight of her. Mrs Wernham, going round behind the chairs with a large black teapot, halting slightly in her walk, was not aware of her for a moment. Then she turned suddenly.

'Oh, is it Madam!' she exclaimed. 'Come in, then, come in! We're at tea.' And she dragged forward a chair.

'No, I won't come in,' said Isabel. 'I'm afraid I interrupt your meal.'

'No – no – not likely, Madam, not likely.'

'Hasn't Mr Pervin come in, do you know?'

'I'm sure I couldn't say! Missed him, have you Madam?'

'No, I only wanted him to come in,' laughed Isabel, as if shyly.

'Wanted him, did ye? Get up, boy – get up, now –'

Mrs Wernham knocked one of the boys on the shoulder. He began to scrape to his feet, chewing largely.

'I believe he's in top stable,' said another face from the table.

'Ah! No, don't get up. I'm going myself,' said Isabel.

'Don't you go out of a dirty night like this. Let the lad go. Get along wi' ye, boy,' said Mrs Wernham.

'No, no,' said Isabel, with a decision that was always obeyed. 'Go on with your tea, Tom. I'd like to go across to the stable, Mrs Wernham.'

'Did ever you hear tell!' exclaimed the woman.

'Isn't the trap late?' asked Isabel.

'Why, no,' said Mrs Wernham, peering into the distance at the tall, dim clock. 'No, Madam – we can give it another quarter or twenty minutes yet, good – yes, every bit of a quarter.'

'Ah! It seems late when darkness falls so early,' said Isabel.

'It do, that it do. Bother the days, that they draw in so,' answered Mrs Wernham. 'Proper miserable!'

'They are,' said Isabel, withdrawing.

She pulled on her overshoes, wrapped a large tartan shawl around her, put on a man's felt hat, and ventured out along the causeways of the first yard. It was very dark. The wind was roaring in the great elms behind the outhouses. When she came to the second yard the darkness seemed deeper. She was unsure of her footing. She wished she had brought a lantern. Rain blew against her. Half she liked it, half she felt unwilling to battle.

She reached at last the just visible door of the stable. There was no sign of a light anywhere. Opening the upper half, she looked in: into a simple well of darkness. The smell of horses, and ammonia, and of warmth was startling to her, in that full night. She listened with all her ears, but could hear nothing save the night, and the stirring of a horse.

'Maurice!' she called, softly and musically, though she was afraid. 'Maurice – are you there?'

Nothing came from the darkness. She knew the rain and wind blew in upon the horses, the hot animal life. Feeling it wrong, she entered the stable, and drew the lower half of the door shut, holding the upper part close. She did not stir, because she was aware of the presence of the dark hind-quarters of the horses, though she could not see them, and she was afraid. Something wild stirred in her heart.

She listened intensely. Then she heard a small noise in the distance – far away, it seemed – the chink of a pan, and a man's voice speaking a brief word. It would be Maurice, in the other part of the stable. She stood motionless, waiting for him to come through the partition door. The horses were so terrifyingly near to her, in the invisible.

The loud jarring of the inner door-latch made her start; the door was opened. She could hear and feel her husband entering and invisibly passing among the horses near to her, in darkness as they were, actively intermingled. The rather low sound of his voice as he spoke to the horses came velvety to her nerves. How near he was, and how invisible! The darkness seemed to be in a strange swirl of violent life, just upon her. She turned giddy.

Her presence of mind made her call, quietly and musically:
'Maurice! Maurice – dea-ar!'

'Yes,' he answered. 'Isabel?'

She saw nothing, and the sound of his voice seemed to touch her.

'Hello!' she answered cheerfully, straining her eyes to see him. He was still busy, attending to the horses near her, but she saw only darkness. It made her almost desperate.

'Won't you come in, dear?' she said.

'Yes, I'm coming. Just half a minute. *Stand over – now!* Trap's not come, has it?'

'Not yet,' said Isabel.

His voice was pleasant and ordinary, but it had a slight suggestion of the stable to her. She wished he would come away. Whilst he was so utterly invisible she was afraid of him.

'How's the time?' he asked.

'Not yet six,' she replied. She disliked to answer into the dark. Presently he came very near to her, and she retreated out of doors.

'The weather blows in here,' he said, coming steadily forward, feeling for the doors. She shrank away. At last she could dimly see him.

'Bertie won't have much of a drive,' he said, as he closed the doors.

'He won't indeed!' said Isabel calmly, watching the dark shape at the door.

'Give me your arm, dear,' she said.

She pressed his arm close to her, as she went. But she longed to see him, to look at him. She was nervous. He walked erect, with face rather lifted, but with a curious tentative movement of his powerful muscular legs. She could feel the clever, careful, strong contact of his feet with the earth, as she balanced against him. For a moment he was a tower of darkness to her, as if he rose out of the earth.

In the house-passage he wavered, and went cautiously with a curious look of silence about him as he felt for the bench. Then he sat down heavily. He was a man with rather sloping shoulders but with heavy limbs, powerful legs that seemed to know the earth. His head was small, usually carried high and light. As he bent down to unfasten his gaiters and boots he did not look blind. His hair was brown and crisp, his hands were large, reddish, intelligent, the veins stood out in the wrists; and his thighs and knees seemed massive. When he stood up his face and neck were surcharged with blood, the veins stood out on his temples. She did not look at his blindness.

Isabel was always glad when they had passed through the dividing door into their own regions of repose and beauty. She was a little afraid of him, out there in the animal grossness of the back. His bearing also changed, as he smelt the familiar, indefinable odour that pervaded his wife's surroundings, a delicate, refined scent, very faintly spicy. Perhaps it came from the pot-pourri bowls.

He stood at the foot of the stairs, arrested, listening. She watched him, and her heart sickened. He seemed to be listening to fate.

'He's not here yet,' he said. 'I'll go up and change.'

'Maurice,' she said, 'you're not wishing he wouldn't come, are you?'

'I couldn't quite say,' he answered 'I feel myself rather on the *qui vive*.'

'I can see you are,' she answered. And she reached up and kissed his cheek. She saw his mouth relax into a slow smile.

'What are you laughing at?' she said roguishly.

'You consoling me,' he answered.

'Nay,' she answered. 'Why should I console you? You know we love each other – you know *how* married we are! What does anything else matter?'

'Nothing at all, my dear.'

He felt for her face, and touched it, smiling.

'*You're* all right, aren't you?' he asked, anxiously.

'I'm wonderfully all right, love,' she answered. 'It's you I am a little troubled about, at times.'

'Why me?' he said, touching her cheeks delicately with the tips of his fingers. The touch had an almost hypnotising effect on her.

He went away upstairs. She saw him mount into the darkness, unseeing and unchanging. He did not know that the lamps on the upper corridor were unlighted. He went on into the darkness with unchanging step. She heard him in the bathroom.

Pervin moved about almost unconsciously in his familiar surroundings, dark though everything was. He seemed to know the presence of objects before he touched them. It was a pleasure to him to rock thus through a world of things, carried on the flood in a sort of blood-prescience. He did not think much or trouble much. So long as he kept this sheer immediacy of blood-contact with the substantial world he was happy, he wanted no intervention of visual consciousness. In this state there was a certain rich positivity, bordering sometimes on rapture. Life seemed to move in him like a tide lapping, and advancing, enveloping all things darkly. It was a pleasure to stretch forth the hand and meet the unseen object, clasp it, and possess it in pure contact. He did not try to remember, to visualise. He did not want to. The new way of consciousness substituted itself in him.

The rich suffusion of this state generally kept him happy, reaching its culmination in the consuming passion for his wife. But at times the flow would seem to be checked and thrown back. Then it would beat inside him like a tangled sea, and he was tortured in the shattered chaos of his own blood. He grew to dread this arrest, this throw-back, this chaos inside himself, when he seemed merely at the mercy of his own powerful and conflicting elements. How to get some measure of control or surety, this was the question. And when the question rose maddening in him, he would clench his fists as if he would *compel* the whole universe to submit to him. But it was in vain. He could not even compel himself.

Tonight, however, he was still serene, though little tremors of unreasonable exasperation ran through him. He had to handle the razor very carefully, as he shaved, for it was not at one with him, he was afraid of it. His hearing also was too much sharpened. He heard the woman lighting the lamps on the corridor, and attending to the fire in the visitor's room. And then, as he went to his room he heard the trap arrive. Then came Isabel's voice, lifted and calling, like a bell ringing:

'Is it you, Bertie? Have you come?'

And a man's voice answered out of the wind:

'Hello, Isabel! There you are.'

'Have you had a miserable drive? I'm so sorry we couldn't send a closed carriage. I can't see you at all, you know.'

'I'm coming. No, I liked the drive – it was like Perthshire. Well, how are you? You're looking fit as ever, as far as I can see.'

'Oh, yes,' said Isabel. 'I'm wonderfully well. How are you? Rather thin, I think –'

'Worked to death – everybody's old cry. But I'm all right, Ciss. How's Pervin? – isn't he here?'

'Oh, yes, he's upstairs changing. Yes, he's awfully well. Take off your wet things; I'll send them to be dried.'

'And how are you both, in spirits? He doesn't fret?'

'No – no, not at all. No, on the contrary, really. We've been wonderfully happy, incredibly. It's more than I can understand – so wonderful: the nearness, and the peace –'

'Ah! Well, that's awfully good news—'

They moved away. Pervin heard no one. But a childish sense of desolation had come over him, as he heard their brisk voices. He seemed shut out – like a child that is left out. He was aimless and excluded, he did not know what to do with himself. The helpless desolation came over him. He fumbled nervously as he dressed himself, in a state almost of childishness. He disliked the Scotch accent in Bertie's speech, and the slight response it found on Isabel's tongue. He disliked the slight purr of complacency in the Scottish speech. He disliked intensely the glib way in which Isabel spoke of their happiness and nearness. It made him recoil. He was fretful and beside himself like a child, he had almost a childish nostalgia to be included in the life circle. And at the same time he was a man, dark and powerful and infuriated by his own weakness. By some fatal flaw, he could not be by himself, he had to depend on the support of another. And this very dependence enraged him. He hated Bertie Reid, and at the same time he knew the hatred was nonsense, he knew it was the outcome of his own weakness.

He went downstairs. Isabel was alone in the dining-room. She watched him enter, head erect, his feet tentative. He looked so strong-blooded and healthy, and, at the same time, cancelled. Cancelled – that was the word that flew across her mind. Perhaps it was his scars suggested it.

'You heard Bertie come, Maurice?' she said.

'Yes – isn't he here?'

'He's in his room. He looks very thin and worn.'

'I suppose he works himself to death.'

A woman came in with a tray – and after a few minutes Bertie came down. He was a little dark man, with a very big forehead, thin, wispy hair, and sad, large eyes. His expression was inordinately sad – almost funny. He had odd, short legs.

Isabel watched him hesitate under the door, and glance nervously at her husband. Pervin heard him and turned.

'Here you are, now,' said Isabel. 'Come, let us eat.'

Bertie went across to Maurice.

'How are you, Pervin,' he said, as he advanced.

The blind man stuck his hand out into space, and Bertie took it.

'Very fit. Glad you've come,' said Maurice.

Isabel glanced at them, and glanced away, as if she could not bear to see them.

'Come,' she said. 'Come to table. Aren't you both awfully hungry? I am, tremendously.'

'I'm afraid you waited for me,' said Bertie, as they sat down.

Maurice had a curious monolithic way of sitting in a chair, erect and distant. Isabel's heart always beat when she caught sight of him thus.

'No,' she replied to Bertie. 'We're very little later than usual. We're having a sort of high tea, not dinner. Do you mind? It gives us such a nice long evening, uninterrupted.'

'I like it,' said Bertie.

Maurice was feeling, with curious little movements, almost like a cat kneading her bed, for his place, his knife and fork, his napkin. He was getting the whole geography of his cover into his consciousness. He sat erect and inscrutable, remote-seeming. Bertie watched the static figure of the blind man, the delicate tactile discernment of the large, ruddy hands, and the curious mindless silence of the brow, above the scar. With difficulty he looked away, and without knowing what he did, picked up a little crystal bowl of violets from the table, and held them to his nose.

'They are sweet-scented,' he said. 'Where do they come from?'

'From the garden – under the windows,' said Isabel.

'So late in the year – and so fragrant! Do you remember the violets under Aunt Bell's south wall?'

The two friends looked at each other and exchanged a smile, Isabel's eyes lighting up.

'Don't I?' she replied. '*Wasn't* she queer!'

'A curious old girl,' laughed Bertie. 'There's a streak of freakishness in the family, Isabel.'

'Ah – but not in you and me, Bertie,' said Isabel. 'Give them to Maurice, will you?' she added, as Bertie was putting down the flowers. 'Have you smelled the violets, dear? Do! – they are so scented.'

Maurice held out his hand, and Bertie placed the tiny bowl against his large, warm-looking fingers. Maurice's hand closed over the thin white fingers of the barrister. Bertie carefully extricated himself. Then the two watched the blind man smelling the violets. He bent his head and seemed to be thinking. Isabel waited.

'Aren't they sweet, Maurice?' she said at last, anxiously.

'Very,' he said. And he held out the bowl. Bertie took it. Both he and Isabel were a little afraid, and deeply disturbed.

The meal continued. Isabel and Bertie chatted spasmodically. The blind man was silent. He touched his food repeatedly, with quick, delicate touches of his knife-point, then cut irregular bits. He could not bear to be helped. Both Isabel and Bertie suffered : Isabel wondered why. She did not suffer when she was alone with Maurice. Bertie made her conscious of a strangeness.

After the meal the three drew their chairs to the fire, and sat down to talk. The decanters were put on a table near at hand. Isabel knocked the logs on the fire, and clouds of brilliant sparks went up the chimney. Bertie noticed a slight weariness in her bearing.

'You will be glad when your child comes now, Isabel?' he said.

She looked up to him with a quick wan smile.

'Yes, I shall be glad,' she answered. 'It begins to seem long. Yes, I shall be very glad. So will you, Maurice, won't you?' she added.

'Yes, I shall,' replied her husband.

'We are both looking forward so much to having it,' she said.

'Yes, of course,' said Bertie.

He was a bachelor, three or four years older than Isabel. He lived in beautiful rooms overlooking the river, guarded by a faithful Scottish man-servant. And he had his friends among the fair sex – not lovers, friends. So long as he could avoid any danger of courtship or marriage, he adored a few good women with constant and unfailing homage, and he was chivalrously fond of quite a number. But if they seemed to encroach on him, he withdrew and detested them.

Isabel knew him very well, knew his beautiful constancy, and kindness, also his incurable weakness, which made him unable ever to enter into close contact of any sort. He was ashamed of himself, because he could not marry, could not approach women physically. He wanted to do so. But he could not. At the centre of him he was afraid, helplessly and even brutally afraid. He had given up hope, had ceased to expect any more that he could escape his own weakness. Hence he was a brilliant and successful barrister, also *littérateur* of high repute, a rich man, and a great social success. At the centre he felt himself neuter, nothing.

Isabel knew him well. She despised him even while she admired him. She looked at his sad face, his little short legs, and felt contempt of him. She looked at his dark grey eyes, with their uncanny, almost childlike intuition, and she loved him. He understood amazingly – but she had no fear of his understanding. As a man she patronised him.

And she turned to the impassive, silent figure of her husband. He sat leaning back, with folded arms, and face a little uptilted. His knees were straight and massive. She sighed, picked up the poker, and again began to prod the fire, to rouse the clouds of soft, brilliant sparks.

'Isabel tells me,' Bertie began suddenly, 'that you have not suffered unbearably from the loss of sight.'

Maurice straightened himself to attend, but kept his arms folded.

'No,' he said, 'not unbearably. Now and again one struggles against it, you know. But there are compensations.'

'They say it is much worse to be stone deaf,' said Isabel.

'I believe it is,' said Bertie. 'Are there compensations?' he added, to Maurice.

'Yes. You cease to bother about a great many things.' Again Maurice stretched his figure, stretched the strong muscles of his back, and leaned backwards, with uplifted face.

'And that is a relief,' said Bertie. 'But what is there in place of the bothering? What replaces the activity?'

There was a pause. At length the blind man replied, as out of a negligent, unattentive thinking:

'Oh, I don't know. There's a good deal when you're not active.'

'Is there?' said Bertie. 'What, exactly? It always seems to me that when there is no thought and no action, there is nothing.'

Again Maurice was slow in replying.

'There is something,' he replied. 'I couldn't tell you what it is.'

And the talk lapsed once more, Isabel and Bertie chatting gossip and reminiscence, the blind man silent.

At length Maurice rose restlessly, a big, obtrusive figure. He felt tight and hampered. He wanted to go away.

'Do you mind,' he said, 'if I go and speak to Wernham?'

'No – go along, dear,' said Isabel.

And he went out. A silence came over the two friends. At length Bertie said:

'Nevertheless, it is a great deprivation, Cissie.'

'It is, Bertie. I know it is.'

'Something lacking all the time,' said Bertie.

'Yes, I know. And yet – and yet – Maurice is right. There is something else, something *there*, which you never knew was there, and which you can't express.'

'What is there?' asked Bertie.

'I don't know – it's awfully hard to define it – but something strong and immediate. There's something strange in Maurice's presence – indefinable – but I couldn't do without it. I agree that it seems to put one's mind to sleep. But when we're alone I miss nothing; it seems awfully rich, almost splendid, you know.'

'I'm afraid I don't follow,' said Bertie.

They talked desultorily. The wind blew loudly outside, rain chattered on the window-panes, making a sharp, drum-sound, because of the closed, mellow-golden shutters inside. The logs burned slowly, with hot, almost invisible small flames. Bertie seemed uneasy, there were dark circles round his eyes. Isabel, rich with her approaching maternity, leaned looking into the fire. Her hair curled in odd, loose strands, very pleasing to the man. But she had a curious feeling of old woe in her heart, old, timeless night-woe.

'I suppose we're all deficient somewhere,' said Bertie.

'I suppose so,' said Isabel wearily.

'Damned, sooner or later.'

'I don't know,' she said, rousing herself. 'I feel quite all right, you know. The child coming seems to make me indifferent to everything, just placid. I can't feel that there's anything to trouble about, you know.'

'A good thing, I should say,' he replied slowly.

'Well, there it is. I suppose it's just Nature. If only I felt I needn't trouble about Maurice, I should be perfectly content –'

'But you feel you must trouble about him?'

'Well – I don't know –' She even resented this much effort.

The evening passed slowly. Isabel looked at the clock. 'I say,' she said. 'It's nearly ten o'clock. Where can Maurice be? I'm sure they're all in bed at the back. Excuse me a moment.'

She went out, returning almost immediately.

'It's all shut up and in darkness,' she said. 'I wonder where he is. He must have gone out to the farm –'

Bertie looked at her.

'I suppose he'll come in,' he said.

'I suppose so,' she said. 'But it's unusual for him to be out now.'

'Would you like me to go out and see?'

'Well – if you wouldn't mind. I'd go, but –' She did not want to make the physical effort.

Bertie put on an old overcoat and took a lantern. He went out from the side door. He shrank from the wet and roaring night. Such weather had a nervous effect on him: too much moisture everywhere made him feel almost imbecile. Unwilling, he went through it all. A dog barked violently at him. He peered in all the buildings. At last, as he opened the upper door of a sort of intermediate barn, he heard a grinding noise, and looking in, holding up his lantern, saw Maurice, in his shirt-sleeves, standing listening, holding the handle of a turnip-pulper. He had been pulping sweet roots, a pile of which lay dimly heaped in a corner behind him.

'That you, Wernham?' said Maurice, listening.

'No, it's me,' said Bertie.

A large, half-wild grey cat was rubbing at Maurice's leg. The blind man stooped to rub its side. Bertie watched the scene, then unconsciously entered and shut the door behind him. He was in a high sort of barn-place, from which, right and left, ran off the corridors in front of the stalled cattle. He watched the slow, stooping motion of the other man, as he caressed the great cat.

Maurice straightened himself.

'You came to look for me?' he said.

'Isabel was a little uneasy,' said Bertie.

'I'll come in. I like messing about doing these jobs.'

The cat had reared her sinister, feline length against his leg, clawing at his thigh affectionately. He lifted her claws out of his flesh.

'I hope I'm not in your way at all at the Grange here,' said Bertie, rather shy and stiff.

'My way? No, not a bit. I'm glad Isabel has somebody to talk to. I'm afraid it's I who am in the way. I know I'm not very lively company. Isabel's all right, don't you think? She's not unhappy, is she?'

'I don't think so.'

'What does she say?'

'She says she's very content — only a little troubled about you.'

'Why me?'

'Perhaps afraid that you might brood,' said Bertie, cautiously.

'She needn't be afraid of that.' He continued to caress the flattened grey head of the cat with his fingers. 'What I am a bit afraid of,' he resumed, 'is that she'll find me a dead weight, always alone with me down here.'

'I don't think you need think that,' said Bertie, though this was what he feared himself.

'I don't know,' said Maurice. 'Sometimes I feel it isn't fair that she's saddled with me.' Then he dropped his voice curiously. 'I say,' he asked, secretly struggling, 'is my face much disfigured? Do you mind telling me?'

'There is the scar,' said Bertie, wondering. 'Yes, it is a disfigurement. But more pitiable than shocking.'

'A pretty bad scar, though,' said Maurice.

'Oh, yes.'

There was a pause.

'Sometimes I feel I am horrible,' said Maurice, in a low voice, talking as if to himself. And Bertie actually felt a quiver of horror.

'That's nonsense,' he said.

Maurice again straightened himself, leaving the cat.

'There's no telling,' he said. Then again, in an odd tone, he added : 'I don't really know you, do I?'

'Probably not,' said Bertie.

'Do you mind if I touch you?'

The lawyer shrank away instinctively. And yet, out of very philanthropy, he said, in a small voice, 'Not at all.'

But he suffered as the blind man stretched out a strong, naked hand to him. Maurice accidentally knocked off Bertie's hat.

'I thought you were taller,' he said starting. Then he laid his hand on Bertie Reid's head, closing the dome of the skull in a soft, firm grasp, gathering it, as it were; then, shifting his grasp and softly closing again, with a fine, close pressure, till he had covered the skull and the face of the smaller man, tracing the brows, and touching the full, closed eyes, touching the small nose and the nostrils, the rough, short moustache, the mouth, the rather strong chin. The hand of the blind man grasped the shoulder, the arm, the hand of the other man. He seemed to take him, in the soft, travelling grasp.

'You seem young,' he said quietly, at last.

The lawyer stood almost annihilated, unable to answer.

'Your head seems tender, as if you were young,' Maurice repeated. 'So do your hands. Touch my eyes, will you? – touch my scar.'

Now Bertie quivered with revulsion. Yet he was under the power of the blind man, as if hypnotised. He lifted his hand, and laid the fingers on the scar, on the scarred eyes. Maurice suddenly covered them with his own hand, pressed the fingers of the other man upon his disfigured eye-sockets, trembling in every fibre, and rocking slightly, slowly, from side to side. He remained thus for a minute or more, whilst Bertie stood as if in a swoon, unconscious, imprisoned.

Then suddenly Maurice removed the hand of the other man from his brow, and stood holding it in his own.

'Oh, my God,' he said, 'we shall know each other now, shan't we? We shall know each other now.'

Bertie could not answer. He gazed mute and terror-struck, overcome by his own weakness. He knew he could not answer. He had an unreasonable fear, lest the other man should suddenly destroy him. Whereas Maurice was actually filled with hot, poignant love, the passion of friendship. Perhaps it was this very passion of friendship which Bertie shrank from most.

'We're all right together now, aren't we?' said Maurice. 'It's all right now, as long as we live, so far as we're concerned?'

'Yes,' said Bertie, trying by any means to escape.

Maurice stood with head lifted, as if listening. The new delicate fulfilment of mortal friendship had come as a revelation and surprise to him, something exquisite and unhoped-for. He seemed to be listening to hear if it were real.

Then he turned for his coat.

'Come,' he said, 'we'll go to Isabel.'

Bertie took the lantern and opened the door. The cat disappeared. The two men went in silence along the causeways. Isabel, as they came, thought their footsteps sounded strange. She looked up pathetically and anxiously for their entrance. There seemed a curious elation about Maurice. Bertie was haggard, with sunken eyes.

'What is it?' she asked.

'We've become friends,' said Maurice, standing with his feet apart, like a strange colossus.

'Friends!' re-echoed Isabel. And she looked again at Bertie. He met her eyes with a furtive, haggard look; his eyes were as if glazed with misery.

'I'm so glad,' she said, in sheer perplexity.

'Yes,' said Maurice.

He was indeed so glad. Isabel took his hand with both hers, and held it fast.

'You'll be happier now, dear,' she said.

But she was watching Bertie. She knew that he had one desire – to escape from this intimacy, this friendship, which had been thrust upon him. He could not bear it that he had been touched by the blind man, his insane reserve broken in. He was like a mollusc whose shell is broken.

Notes and References

Introduction

1. The following anthologies provide a fair introduction to the variety of approaches attempted to date and I have generally referred the reader to them rather than to other sources which might prove relatively inaccessible: *Style in Language*, ed. Thomas Sebeok, The Technology Press/Wiley, 1960; *Essays in Style and Language*, ed. Roger Fowler, Routledge and Kegan Paul, 1966; *Contemporary Essays on Style*, ed. Glen A. Love and Michael Payne, Scott, Foresman, 1969; *Linguistics and Literary Style*, Donald C. Freeman, Holt, Rinehart and Winston, 1970; *Literary Style: A Symposium*, ed. Seymour Chatman, Oxford University Press, 1971; *Essays in Stylistic Analysis*, ed. Howard S. Babb, Harcourt Brace Jovanovich, 1971; *Current Trends in Stylistics*, Linguistic Research Inc., 1972. (The anthologies are referred to hereafter as ' Sebeok anthology ', ' Fowler anthology ', etc.) The reader will also find the following useful: *A Critical Bibliography of the New Stylistics Applied to the Romance Literatures, 1953-1965*, Helmut Hatzfeld, Chapel Hill, 1966, and *English Stylistics: A Bibliography*, Richard W. Bailey and Dolores M. Burton, M.I.T. Press, 1968; also the magazines *Style*, Fayetteville, Arkansas, 1967-, *Language and Style*, Southern Illinois University, 1968-.

See also the general discussion of linguistics, stylistics and criticism in Roger Fowler's *The Languages of Literature*, Routledge and Kegan Paul, 1971, which includes a discussion with F. W. Bateson reprinted from *Essays in Criticism*, 1967 and 1968. Some of the issues discussed were raised in *The Times Literary Supplement*, in a correspondence following Geoffrey Leech's article, ' The Linguistic and the Literary ' (23.7.70): *To the Editor*, 31.7.70, 14.8.70, 28.8.70, 4.9.70 and 11.9.70.

2. See the brief but pointed discussion of practical criticism in Ian Watt's 'The First Paragraph of the Ambassadors: An Explication', reprinted from *Essays in Criticism*, July 1960, in Love and Payne anthology, pp. 266–283.

3. The latter approach is, in fact, the most widespread. It is illustrated, from different angles, by Josephine Miles' *The Continuity of Poetic Language*, Octagon Books, 1965, by Geoffrey Leech in *A Linguistic Guide to English Poetry*, Longmans, 1969, and by Crystal and Davy in *Investigating English Style*, Longmans, 1969. The anthologies already cited all contain papers of interest in this connection. Three of the best known are Richard Ohmann's 'Modes of Order' and 'Generative Grammars and the Concept of Style', Freeman anthology, pp. 209-242 and 258-278 respectively, and M. A. K. Halliday's 'Linguistic Function and Literary Style, an Enquiry into the Language of William Golding's *The Inheritors*', Chatman anthology, pp. 330-368. Related problems are discussed by Louis T. Milic, 'Against the Typology of Styles', Love and Payne anthology, pp. 283-292. (See also note 23 in p. 136 below.) See also Pierre Guiraud, 'Imminence and Transitivity of Stylistic Criteria', Chatman anthology, pp. 16-28, and subsequent discussion.

4. See similarly Edward Stankiewicz, 'Linguistics and the Study of Poetic Language', Sebeok anthology, pp. 69–81, especially 'Meaning . . . far from being extrinsic to the study of poetic language, can be analysed and explained only with relation to other elements of poetic organisation'. This is also, for example, Roger Fowler's opinion, e.g. *The Languages of Literature*, p. 38ff.

5. The linguistic analysis that I have myself used as a basis of description is that proposed by Scale and Category grammar, familiar to many British students of linguistics and relatively easy to handle if one comes to modern linguistics from traditional English grammar. It offers a convenient way of describing the 'surface' patterns that occur in the chain of speech. The associated descriptive technique seldom appears explicitly, however, in this book, so that an introduction to it will not be found a necessary adjunct to reading these studies. The reader may find useful the chapter on 'Linguistic Description' in Crystal and Davy, op. cit., pp. 15-59.

6. The more fully this can be done, the better. As Edward Stankiewicz wrote in the article cited above (note 4), 'it is quite

clear that the study of verbal art is intrinsically connected with, and must be based on, the study of language – the linguist's discipline' (p. 69).

7. This was well brought out in the discussions between F. W. Bateson and others which took place a few years ago. (See Fowler, *The Languages of Literature*, and the *T.L.S.* correspondence already referred to in note 1 above.)

8. See especially Michael A. K. Halliday, ' Linguistic Function and Literary Style ', Freeman anthology, pp. 330-365 and following discussion.

9. See Roman Jakobson, ' Poetry of Grammar and Grammar of Poetry ', *Lingua* (68), where, despite the congenial description of what so often happens in stylistic work, the issue of relevance is not much clarified : ' Any unbiased, attentive, exhaustive, total description of the selection, distribution and interrelation of diverse morphological classes and syntactic constructions in a given poem surprise the examiner himself by the unexpected striking symmetries and antisymmetries, balanced structure, efficient accumulation of equivalent forms and salient contrasts, finally by rigid restrictions in the repertory of morphological and syntactic constituents used in the poem, eliminations which, on the other hand, permit us to follow the masterly interplay of the actualised constituents. Let us insist on the strikingness of these devices; any sensitive reader, as Sapir would say, feels instinctively the poetic effect and the semantic load of these grammatical appliances, " without the slightest attempt at conscious analysis ", and in many cases the poet himself in this respect is similar to such a reader.' It has been pointed out by critics of Jakobson's brilliant stylistic analyses that there are a potentially infinite number of formal interrelations in any text, so that issues of selection and therefore relevance are plainly crucial and ought if possible to be made conscious. See, for example, Michael Riffaterre, ' Describing Poetic Structures: Two Approaches to Baudelaire's " Les Chats " ', Babb anthology, pp. 362-392.

10. This applies both to general stylistic criteria, such as might guide a critic in his approach to any text whatever, and to the particular considerations that might be expected to affect his description of unique interrelationships of linguistic features in a given work. It is with the latter that this book is generally concerned.

11. Similarly Michael Riffaterre in ' Criteria of Style Analysis ',

Word (5), 1959, p. 154 : 'A purely linguistic analysis of a work of literature will yield only linguistic elements; it will describe those elements of sequence which happen to have a stylistic value along with the central ones.' As will become apparent, however, I do not follow Riffaterre in so far as his formulation implies that linguistic analysis will *at least* provide us with all the features amongst which we must choose and that stylistic value is an attribute of some linguistic features regardless of their unique contexts in given works.

12. See, however, Michael Halliday's flexible response, typified by his comment that 'Linguistics is not and never will be the whole of literary analysis, and only the literary analyst – not the linguist – can determine the place of linguistics in literary studies'. ('Descriptive Linguistics in Literary Studies', *Patterns of Language*, ed. A. McIntosh and M. A. K. Halliday, Longmans, 1966, p. 67.) Roger Fowler makes the same point in 'Linguistics, Stylistics; Criticism?', *The Languages of Literature*, pp. 32-42.

13. This is an area in which public debate is now indispensable.

14. Compare Sol Saporta's approach in 'The Application of Linguistics to the Study of Poetic Language', Sebeok anthology, pp. 82-93 : 'The linguist cannot study poetry as an art without abandoning his position as linguist.' Although it seems true to say that some of the stylistician's work on texts will take him beyond the present *and proper* boundaries of linguistics, other aspects of his work might well come to be regarded as a *valid extension* of the linguist's investigation of 'how language works'. (See brief discussion in Chapter 5, pp. 110-111.)

15. A simple visual illustration is the shape whose orientation can be seen as oscillating :

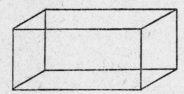

16. See some interesting work recorded, for example, in *Psychological and Psychiatric Aspects of Speech and Hearing*, ed. Dominick A. Barbara, Springfield, Illinois, Thomas, 1960.

17. See the discussion by J. Tynianov, 'La Notion de Construction', *Théorie de la Littérature*, ed. Tzvetan Todorov, Éditions du Seuil, 114-117.

18.   See. for instance. the discussion of D. H. Lawrence's poem, *Gloire de Dijon*, Chapter 3, pp. 63-68, especially of the effect of the rhyme *mellow* in line 6.

19.   The point is indeed central to the approach adopted in this book, as is that made by the following sentence. The reader will find it worthwhile to consider the textual discussions in Chapters 3 and 4 from this functional point of view. Although precisely the same linguistic features seldom recur in two different texts, unless the texts are deliberately written for the purpose, it is often clear that *similar* features, such as rhyme, have very *different* effects in different texts (e.g. rhyme in *Gloire de Dijon* and *The Falcon*, discussed in Chapter 3) while *different* linguistic features may fulfil *similar* roles in different texts (so that rhyme *or* syntactical recurrences may serve as means of linkage, for example). It may well be that the various linguistic means used for similar purposes may be conditioned by the length of the text, by whether it is intended to be heard or read, and so on; there is here a promising area for future research. Clearly, for the creative writer, this must be a central area of concern. And for the critic, it is this aspect of literary works that makes it necessary to treat every work as a unique whole built up out of unique interrelationships. Hence the incomplete nature of the type of approach illustrated by the work referred to in note 3 above, however essential it may be to the study of whole works: its incompleteness is often partially hidden by the instinctive use stylisticians make of their response to the work in its entirety, though in Halliday's discussion of *The Inheritors* this factor is well brought out, and enters consciously into the method of approach. For an interesting attempt to exclude reference to the whole of the text, see J. McH. Sinclair's ' Taking a Poem to Pieces ', Freeman anthology, pp. 129-142. A completer study of Larkin's *First Sight* would, in my view, have to include acknowledgement of what leads us to find (as I think we do) the syntactical patterns analysed by John Sinclair relevant to the communicative event as a whole. Merely *linguistic* criteria cannot lead us to select these (rather than other) linguistic features for special comment, so that although the linguistic description may be stylistically ' neutral ' in itself, the initial selection of features for discussion, and their eventual incorporation in a total study of the poem, cannot be. However, stylistic selection, carried out with the whole text in mind, is still not *evaluation* though it may provide *some* of the basic ' facts ' on which evaluation is based,

others being of a purely aesthetic or social nature (see also a brief discussion in the final chapter). The utmost interest attaches to studies, like Sinclair's, which attempt, and provoke, a more rigorous exploration of such issues than is appropriate here.

20. See David Katz, *Gestalt Psychology* (transl. Tyson), Methuen, 1950: 'Gestalt psychology rejects the view that sense organs respond to local stimuli with local impressions that are unrelated to other stimuli. Its firm conviction is that the organism reacts as a whole to any given stimulus constellation' (p. 49). Although the gestaltist approach to perception is by no means fully acceptable nowadays (see Bruno Petermann, *The Gestalt Theory*, University of Kiel, Kegan Paul, 1932, for some basic early doubts), it is clear that the notion that perception of detail is influenced by context (formal or semantic) has remained an important one for modern perceptual psychology (see various references to this area in M. D. Vernon's *The Psychology of Perception*, Pelican, 1962). Unfortunately, the research into its application to language-events is not well-developed and certain crucial problems remain unclarified even with respect to visual phenomena; thus, for example, we can be told that deviant features will tend to stand out from their surroundings, but also that they may pass unnoticed because they are unexpected and we tend to interpret according to habit! (A case in point arises in Robert Graves' *Flying Crooked*, where the phrase *here and here* is frequently read as *here and there*, so obliterating an effect which, if the deviation is noticed, contributes to an overall effect created by the convergence of various other linguistic means in the poem.)

21. See the figure on page 32, and discussion pp. 31-32.

22. Of course an emphasis on perception is nothing new in literary criticism, though it has been neglected in a good deal of the linguistic description devoted to literary texts. So Rostrevor Hamilton, in his *Poetry and Contemplation*, Cambridge U.P., 1937, argues that if we hold the belief that there are 'independently real worlds of mind and matter' it may 'reinforce the powerful influence of the notion, dear to common sense, that beauty exists in an object, whether picture or poem, apart from an experiencing mind' (p. 10). His emphasis on the notion that 'each element in the experience of a poem is tinged with the colouring of all the others' (p. 30) derives from his objection to this 'common sense' view. See especially his excellent comments

pp. 64-65. Much of I. A. Richards' most valuable critical work is devoted to an exploration of this area.

23. See an illuminating discussion of related issues in Seymour Chatman's discussion of James Joyce's ' *Eveline* ', *Language and Style*, vol. II, no. 1, 1969, pp. 3-36.

24. This book is concerned with a rather narrow area of the critic's intrinsic concerns. It may be all the more important to insist that extrinsic studies, in the sociology of literature for example, appear to me to be an essential part of critical study and one which is insufficiently developed at present. See the suggestions offered in this area by Raymond Williams, *Culture and Society*, Penguin, 1962 (first published Chatto and Windus, 1958); Ernst Fischer, *The Necessity of Art*, transl. Anna Bostock, Penguin, 1963 (first published in German, 1959); J. M. Hawthorn, *Identity and Relationship*, Lawrence & Wishart, 1973.

25. Chapter 5, pp. 110-111.

26. See also S. R. Levin, ' Internal and External Deviation in Poetry ', *Word*, vol. XXI, no. 2, p. 225 : ' Two aspects of the phenomenon need to be distinguished : the reader-response to certain stretches of language occurring in a poem and the linguistic structure which analysis reveals and which it is claimed stands in some plausible relation to the reader-response.' I do not however follow Levin when he states that ' because deviation is an attribute of form, the interest in responding to it attaches only secondarily to what the deviant expression is saying, but immediately to the expression itself '. Compare the views of Jan Mukařovský, ' Standard Language and Poetic Language ', Freeman anthology, pp. 40-56, and discussion of these, Chapter 3, pp. 59-62.

Chapter 1

1. This is well shown by Dylan Thomas' remarks quoted on pp. 38-39. See also the entirety of ' Notes on the Art of Poetry ', *The Creative Process*, ed. Brewster Ghiselin, Fontana, 1966, pp. 195-204.

A properly functional stylistics has a good deal to offer the writer himself, as I and several colleagues have found in creative writing ' workshops ' both for young people and adults, quite apart from what it has to offer readers in terms of a more intimate understanding of the writer's preoccupations, and the nature and possibilities of the verbal medium.

2.   See however writers' comments recorded in such collections as *Novelists on the Novel*, ed. Miriam Allott, Routledge Paperback, 1959, *Modern Poets on Modern Poetry*, ed. James Scully, Fontana, 1966, *The Creative Process*, ed. Brewster Ghiselin, Fontana, 1966, and, especially interesting for those familiar with French poetry, *Modern French Poets on Poetry*, compiled by Robert Gibson, Cambridge, 1961. See also the 'Writers at Work' series in the *Paris Review*.

3.   Victor Žhirmunský was right to insist (in 1928) on the literal truth that 'the material of poetry is neither images nor emotions, but words . . . Poetry is verbal art'. (Quoted by Victor Erlich, *Russian Formalism*, Mouton, p. 175, a summary of Russian Formalist approaches which is still a quarry of promising suggestions for stylistics.) 'Words' are, of course, meanings as well as forms, and it was one of the Formalists' suggestions that the structuring that goes on in literature affects not only form but also meaning, so that both can be seen as the 'material' of the work, rather than just form (as in more traditional approaches). 'Images' and 'emotions' (in the reader) derive from the words, which are the writer's actual medium and therefore must remain the focus of critical attention. See also John Spencer and Michael J. Gregory, 'An Approach to the Study of Style', Freeman anthology, pp. 73-95, for an attractive delineation of the desirable to-and-fro critical process between form and meaning. Flaubert, in a letter quoted in *Novelists on the Novel*, pp. 313-314, writes : 'You say that I pay too much attention to form. Alas ! it is like body and soul : form and content to me are one; I do not know what either is without the other. The finer the idea, be sure, the finer-sounding the sentence. The exactness of the thought makes for (*and is itself*) that of the word' (my italics). For an interesting general discussion, see René Wellek, 'Concepts of Form and Structure in 20th Century Criticism', *Neophilologus*, 42, 1958, and Gillo Dorflés, 'Pour ou contre une esthétique structuraliste?', *Revue Internationale de Philosophie*, 19, 1965, p. 409ff.

4.   See, as an interesting example of this, Leavis's discussion of Milton's verse in *Revaluation*, aspects of which are discussed in Chapter 3, pp. 53-57.

5.   See, however, discussion of John Sinclair's 'Taking a Poem to Pieces' in note 19, pp. 134-135.

6. See especially David Lodge, *The Language of Fiction*, Routledge and Kegan Paul, 1966.

7. Owen Barfield, in his *Poetic Diction*, Faber and Gwyer, 1928, argues that criticism 'must try to alter the state of mind of the artist's audience, from mere wondering contemplation of an inexplicable *result*, towards something more like sympathetic participation in a *process*' (p. 136). Any critic involved in reviewing contemporary literature will grasp Barfield's point, but it applies equally, I believe, to our understanding of the literature of the past.

8. *The Language Poets Use*, Athlone Press, 1962, p. 24.

9. *Seven Types of Ambiguity*, Chatto & Windus, 1930, p. 12. See also his discussion (pp. 14-15) of the 'scientific' mode of criticism.

10. I have already referred the reader to anthologies of comments by creative writers on the process of composition (note 2, p. 137). In my view, any student of literature should become familiar with this area of his subject and if possible have some first-hand experience of the process. Some British universities acknowledge the value of this aspect of literary studies, following the normal practice of studies in arts such as music, painting, sculpture or architecture. The only real puzzle is why departments of literature have taken so long to begin to include this practical creative aspect of the discipline, and why it has not yet assumed a position of adequate importance. I would suspect that a crucial reason was our poor technical knowledge of the verbal medium, as compared with our knowledge of the media of the other arts.

11. Contrast the view often taken of translation, namely that the better the work, the better it will translate. (See comments on this, and discussion, throughout Chapter 2.)

12. A most lucid and elegant account of this point of view is provided by William Haas in 'Linguistic Relevance', *In Memory of J. R. Firth*, ed. C. E. Bazell, J. C. Catford, M. A. K. Halliday and R. H. Robins, Longmans, 1966, pp. 116-147.

13. The phonemic symbols employed here will be known to many. The reader to whom they are unfamiliar should however have no difficulty in following the points made here, and on a few other occasions when they are used. However, in case of difficulty, he or she may care to refer to A. C. Gimson, *An Introduction to the Pronunciation of English*, Edward Arnold, 1962.

14. W. K. Wimsatt comments on this very pun in *The Verbal Icon*, University of Kentucky Press, 1954, p. 214.

15.   Wimsatt's entire discussion of 'iconic' language is of great interest. The point being made is essentially the same as that made here about the redemption in literature of 'accidents' of language. This formulation derives from an unpublished paper on 'Poetic Licence' given by William Haas to the Linguistics Association of Great Britain. Similar points are made by Professor Haas in *Phono-graphic Translation*, Manchester University Press, 1970, p. 13f.

16.   See the figure on page 32, and discussion.

17.   *The Verbal Icon*, University of Kentucky Press, 1954, p. 231.

18.   See David Lodge on the translation of poetry and of prose, op. cit., pp. 23-26. Certainly there are problems in the translation of poetry that may not arise in the translation of prose (depending on the type of prose, and of poetry, in question), but I suspect that the differences between the two types of translation may have been exaggerated in the past, due to our poor knowledge of the workings of prose.

19.   See Guy de Maupassant, quoted Allott, op. cit., pp. 317-318. Also Fatiano Slama-Cazacu, *Langage et Contexte*, Mouton, 1961 : 'La réalité étant dynamique, le langage, qui doit l'exprimer, ne peut être statique, ne peut employer uniquement des mots à valeurs immuables.' Indeed, each new context into which a word fits is *liable* to shift the word's meaning; and a writer in search of exact expression, of 'reality', will extend the previously-accepted uses of words. (See Chapter 2.)

20.   See Elizabeth Brock-Sulzer, 'The Poet at War with His Language: Remarks on the Newer French Lyric', Babb anthology, pp. 250-274.

21.   Compare W. B. Yeats' well-known remark that, during textual revision, 'it is myself that I remake'.

22.   Quoted in B. Ghiselin, op. cit., p. 179. The following passages are also from *The Creative Process*.

23.   Arthur Koestler, in *The Act of Creation*, makes the point that creation can be seen as the discovery not of new elements but of new combinations of known elements. Similarly, on the plane of imagery, Victor Žhirmunský argues that the poet does not so much 'create' as 'find' images (see Erlich, op. cit., pp. 175-176).

24.   Benjamin Lee Whorf, 'Language, Mind and Reality', *Language, Thought and Reality*, Massachusetts Institute of Technology, 1956, p. 252. Ludwig Bertalanffy, in 'The Mind-

Body Problem : A New View ', *Psychosomatic Medicine*, xxiv, 1964, has interesting things to say on the issues raised by such an approach to human consciousness. The article is reprinted in *The Human Dialogue, Perspectives on Communication*, a stimulating collection put together by Floyd M. Matson and Ashley Montagu, The Free Press, New York/Collier-MacMillan, London, 1966. The socio-linguistic implications are by no means obvious, as is well shown by W. Labov, ' The Logic of nonstandard English ', Georgetown Monographs on Language and Linguistics (1969), reprinted in *Language in Education*, Routledge & Kegan Paul, 1972.

25.   William Haas, ' The Theory of Translation ', *Philosophy*, vol. xxxvi, p. 208. Reprinted in Parkinson, *The Theory of Meaning*, Oxford U.P., 1969.

26.   Quoted Allott, op. cit., p. 319.

27.   Henry James expresses this in his image of the ' house of fiction ', quoted Allott, op. cit., pp. 131-132.

28.   William McDougall's phrase, *An Outline of Psychology*, Methuen, 1923, p. 223, though more recent psychologists would doubt whether he was correct to add ' a passive selection, like that of a sieve '.

29.   Introduction, *The Poems of Vasco Popa*, Penguin, 1969, p. 10.

30.   See Halliday's study referred to above (note 3, p. 131).

31.   There are some brief comments on this in Chapter 4 (pp. 90-92).

32.   Wallace Stevens, *Collected Poems*, Faber and Faber, 1914, ' The Latest Freed Man ', pp. 204-205. The whole poem is relevant.

33.   Hence the insistence of the Russian Formalists on the aesthetic value of ' making it strange ', of ' divergence ', of ' impeded form ' (see Erlich, op. cit., pp. 177-178). Also Riffaterre, ' Criteria for Style Analysis ', *Word* (5), 1959, pp. 157 and 171.

34.   Jean Cocteau, *Le Rappel à l'Ordre*, Paris, 1926, pp. 215-216, quoted by Erlich, op. cit., pp. 179-180. See also Shelley, *A Defence of Poetry*, in *Sidney – ' Apology for Poetry ', Shelley – ' Defence of Poetry '* ed. H. A. Needham, Ginn, 1931, pp. 78-79.

35.   *A Defence of Poetry*, H. A. Needham, op. cit., pp. 104-105. The whole essay is of great interest.

36.   As Robert Louis Stevenson observed, ' the derangement of . . . phrases from their (so-called) natural order is luminous for the mind ' (quoted Allott, op. cit., p. 319). Ronald Peacock, in ' From Abstraction to Reality in Modern Science, Art and

Poetry' in *Literature and Science*, Blackwell, 1955, pp. 329-330, wrote : 'Science having become one kind of symbolism amongst others, that of art is now more valid and persuasive than it has been for generations . . . The argument against art from science was always universal explanation of "the facts", which now falls to the ground. The old opposition between the two is replaced by a sense of related and complementary functions, for they each express an aspect of "man-in-the-world".' : See also my own 'Post-culture: Pre-culture?', *British Poetry since 1960*, Carcanet Press, 1972.

37. *The Necessary Angel*, Faber and Faber 1909, 'The Noble Rider and the Sound of Words', p. 33. The whole essay is of great interest.

38. Similarly Stendhal : 'The more one delves into one's soul, the more one dares to express the most secret thought, then the more one shrinks when it is written down, it seems so strange, and it is this strangeness which is its merit' (quoted Allott, op. cit., pp 127-128). The Russian Formalist principle of 'making it strange' seems indicative of a comparably basic awareness of how language works, as against the more superficial 'make it new' of Ezra Pound, though clearly the two principles are related. The poem by Zbigniew Herbert, 'I Would Like to Describe', comes from *Selected Poems*, Penguin, 1968.

39. The same applies to formal features of a traditional, literary kind, as Hardy pointed out when he wrote : 'The whole secret of a living style and the difference between it and a dead style, lies in not having too much style – being in fact a little careless, or rather seeming to be, here and there. It brings wonderful life into the writing :

> A sweet disorder in the dress . . .
> A careless shoe-string, in whose tie
> I see a wild civility,
> Do more bewitch me than when art
> Is too precise in every part.

Otherwise your style is like worn half-pence – all the fresh images rounded off by rubbing, and no crispness at all.

It is, of course, simply a carrying into prose of the knowledge I have acquired in poetry – that inexact rhymes and rhythms now and then are far more pleasing than correct ones.' (Quoted Allott, op. cit., p. 318.) I believe that this principle, so reminiscent of Verlaine's remarks on choosing words and rhythms as if with some imprecision, applies not just (as it so obviously does) to Modernism but, in various ways, to all good writing. In fact, to detect 'imprecision' the reader needs to keep keen his or her sense of 'correctness', a sense we may lose through too *exclusive* an acquaintance with novelty. Hence, perhaps, fluctuations of taste between the two extremes of informality and formality: each is perceived against the background of the other. Though ideally, the work itself can contain both and so keep perception alive within its own controlling interrelationships.

40.   The definition of 'deviation' is problematic, as is that of 'norm'. The difficulties are shared by linguist and stylistician alike. See, for example, Riffaterre, 'Criteria for Style Analysis', *Word* (5), 1959: pp. 167-168. I have assumed, as is customary, that language is rule-governed behaviour and that deviations from familiar usage, though they cannot be statistically defined, are nevertheless intersubjectively perceptible to speakers with the same linguistic competence.

41.   *Collected Poems*, Faber, p. 165.

42.   *The Dubliner* magazine, Dublin, May-June, 1962. See similarly Dorothy Emmet, *Whitehead's Philosophy of Organism*, Macmillan, 1932: 'Whitehead repeatedly insists, mere unbounded creativity can produce nothing. Actuality is always a limitation on pure creativity and as soon as you have limitation, you have decision between alternatives, which means some kind of definite ordering.' This summarises much of what A. N. Whitehead argues in his intriguing discussion of Wordsworth and other writers in *Science and the Modern World*, Cambridge, 1953.

43.   E. H. Gombrich, *Art and Illusion*, fourth edition, 1972, p. 30. The whole book is of the utmost interest to literary criticism. Roland Barthes makes similar points with reference to the selectivity of the writer's view of the world and of the critic's view of the work (*Critique et Vérité*, Editions du Seuil, pp. 71-72). See interesting discussions of related questions throughout the issues of the French magazine *Tel Quel*.

44.   Gombrich, op. cit., p. 73.

45.   Ernst Kris, quoted by Gombrich, op. cit., p. 25.

46.   Quoted by Victor Erlich, op. cit., p. 181. See also Marcel Raymond, 'Le Poète et la Langue', *Trivium*, Jahrgang II, Atlantis Verlag, Zürich, especially his awareness of the problem of whether 'la réalité, en son fond véritable, est saisissable par le moyen du langage, si elle est « commensurable avec le

langage », suivant la formule de Bergson, avec ce qu'il appelle
« le discours »'. Raymond goes on to quote Mallarmé to the
effect that verse ' vous cause cette surprise de n'avoir ouï jamais
tel fragment ordinaire d'élocution, en même temps que la
réminiscence de l'objet nommé baigne dans une neuve atmos-
phère '.

47.   Wallace Stevens, *Collected Poems*, p. 203.

48.   As was suggested in notes 39 and 40 above.

49.   See note 5, p. 131.

50.   Some further discussion of this topic appears in Chapter 5,
pp. 108-109.

51.   See Erlich, op. cit., p. 183. And discussion of Jan
Mukařovský's views, Chapter 3, pp. 59-62.

52.   See interesting discussion, E. Nagel, ' Wholes, Sums and
Organic Unities ', *Philosophical Studies*, vol. III, University of
Minnesota Press, 1952. Winifred Nowottny, op. cit., suggests
that the ' unruffled surface ' of the diction of Pope's *Pastorals* ' is
almost a necessary condition of our being set at ease to follow
the patterns moving beneath it with such agile assurance ' (p. 12):
that is, the syntactic patterns. As Pamela Mason (a student at
Birmingham University) recently pointed out in discussion, the
way in which the lexical-cum-auditory main structure of *Gloire
de Dijon* stands out depends largely on the relative *absence* of
competing auditory patterning. In a subsequent composition
workshop, we had occasion to confirm this, another student
having attempted to reproduce the dominant structure of
Lawrence's poem in one of her own and found that her listeners
were confused, when she read the result aloud, as to which sound
was the crucial one, so that the effects Lawrence gets within his
first verse were lost in hers. (See discussion of *Gloire de Dijon*,
Chapter 3, pp. 63-68). Similarly, Erlich, op. cit., explaining points
made by Roman Ingarden and Roman Jakobson, argues that a
work is not a cluster of devices but ' a complex multi-dimensional
structure integrated by the unity of aesthetic purpose ' (p. 198).
I have reservations about the stress laid here on *aesthetic* purpose,
however, for reasons which have already been partly explained
and which receive further discussion at various points in the
following pages.

53.   See S. R. Levin, *Linguistic Structures in Poetry*, Mouton,
1962, p. 35. Also Riffaterre, ' Criteria for Style Analysis ', *Word*
(5), 1959 on ' convergence '.

54.   This figure was often used by the Gestalt psychologists to

illustrate the influence of the human tendency to 'make sense' of ambiguous figures. Thus if this figure is flashed on a screen accompanied with the label DUCK the audience will tend to draw it afterwards without the dot and with some rearrangement of the shape to fit the label better. And the dot is emphasised if the label RABBIT accompanies the figure. Perception is selective, and may be modified by semantic factors. Another illustration of the influence of context on perception is that of the disappearance of so-called Ehrenfels qualities when context is restricted: a 'cloudy' glass of water will appear just 'grey' if part of it only is seen through a hole in a card, a 'black book in sunlight' will appear just 'pale' under the same conditions – the sense of sunlight on a black surface disappears. Such experiments support the feeling many critics have that the linguistic analysis of a literary text 'destroys' its effect (though it cannot, of course, destroy the text itself, as the emotive formula 'we murder to dissect' may suggest). The remedy is always to bear the whole in mind: not only to 'put the pieces together' but to analyse them *in the first place* with an eye to their function in relation to each other and to the whole.

55. This is the type of consideration which leads me to emphasise the role of rhyme in verses 12-13 of *The Falcon*, and not to stress the deviant phrase 'she drips herself with water' in *Gloire de Dijon* (for both analyses, see Chapter 3). The latter has of course some role to play (in the intensification of effect that constitutes the main development in verse 2 of the poem), but this role is also played by other, textually wider-flung effects: the effect of the phrase at the beginning of verse 2 is to trigger off, perhaps, increased attention, appropriate to the fact that it provides the situational 'justification' for the intenser visual effects that follow, as I suggest (p. 66).

56. If, indeed, there can be said to be such a thing: scale cannot be ignored. A 'dot' the size of a pea will stand out in such a figure – but not if the figure (alone) were enlarged to the size of a mural!

57. See note 15, p. 157.

58. Robert Graves, *Selected Poems*, Penguin, 1961, p. 81. Some printings of this poem have two *the*'s in line 1, some *a* in the place of the second *the*. I have used the former version because it seems to fit in best with other effects throughout the poem, though it is not that which appears in the convenient *Penguin Poets* edition referred to.

59. See Jan Mukařovský, ' L'Art comme fait sémiologique ',
Proceedings of the 8th International Congress of Philosophy,
Prague, 1936. The paper clarifies some of the issues facing any
critic desirous of constructing a theory of literary value based
on individual psychological reactions (and bears on some
of I. A. Richards' unsatisfactory formulations in *Principles of
Literary Criticism*). Mukařovský's appeal to the ' common
denominator ' of collective response is, however, misleading in
its turn. For a neat commentary, see F. E. Spearshott, *The Contexts of Criticism*, Clarendon Press, 1967, p. 105. Also R. Wellek
and A. Warren, *Theory of Literature*, Peregrine Books, 1963,
Chapter 12.

60. Victor Erlich, op. cit., remarks that ' the mechanism of
the esthetic response is a legitimate concern of the " objectivist "
art theoretician, provided that the emphasis is placed not on the
individual reader's idiosyncratic associations, but on the qualities
inherent in the work of art and capable of eliciting " intersubjective " responses ' (p. 178). Again, Leo Spitzer, in *Essays on
English and American Literature*, Princeton University Press,
1962, insists that ' the *concensus omnium* is as much an ideal in
the explanation of poetry as it is in etymological investigation '
(p. 69), but this should not be understood to mean simply the
most *widespread* response : Erlich's formulation makes this
clear.

61. Writing well is therefore a practical and rational process,
however deeply irrational it may also be.

62. My translation, from *Autres Rhumbs*, Paris, 1934, pp.
143-144 :

Je cherche un mot (dit le poète) un mot qui soit
> féminin,
> de deux syllabes,
> contenant P ou F,
> terminé par une muette,
> et synonyme de brisure, désagrégation;
> et pas savant, pas rare.
> Six conditions – au moins !

63. I. A. Richards.

64. An interesting side-light on this issue is provided by Winifred Nowottny, op. cit., when she writes, during the course of a
discussion of Spender's line *Afternoon burns upon the wires of
the sea* : ' We should note that metaphor directs us to the *sense*,
not to the exact term. The directions lead us, not to the term

" ridges ", not to the term " swell ", not to the term " humps ", not to the term " crests ", but to that which in nature is the target of all these verbal shots. By not using any of these terms, metaphor allows us to supply an uncontaminated image from our own experience of the physical world. . . This is why metaphor has physical immediacy ' (p. 59). As it happens, Spender's metaphor does not, for me, have immediacy, but nevertheless I find the general point being made an intriguing one, despite the dubious implications of ' uncontaminated ' (see discussion p. 27ff).

65.   J. R. Firth, *Papers in Linguistics*, Oxford University Press, 1957, p. 184. Also pp. 141-142. See the autobiographical evidence for this provided by Henry Miller, quoted in part, pp. 23-24 above, from Ghiselin, op. cit., pp. 178-185. Firth's statement applies to every speaker of a language, Miller's records the writer's particularly strenuous search for a style.

66.   The complexity of the choices to be made was well described by Lev Jakubinský : ' Man's speech activity is a complex phenomenon. This complexity finds expression not only in the existence of various languages and lingoes, down to the dialects of social groups, and individual idiosyncrasies, but likewise, in functional differences within each of these linguistics systems ' (quoted by Erlich, op. cit., p. 235).

67.   This, indeed, is perhaps the most fundamental effect of studying linguistics, quite apart from any specific analytical tools the discipline may provide.

68.   J. R. Firth, *Papers in Linguistics*, Oxford University Press, 1957, p. 183.

69.   Quoted by Erlich, op. cit., pp. 176-177.

70.   Charles Davy, *Words in the Mind*, Chatto & Windus, 1965, p. 96.

71.   *Defence of Poetry*, op. cit., p. 102.

72.   *Dr Zhivago*, Fontana, 1967, p. 427. The reader may care to refer to *The Poems of Dr Zhivago*, translated with a commentary by D. A. Davie, Manchester, 1965, for some most interesting comments on linguistic issues.

73.   Quoted by Ghiselin, op. cit., p. 200. The whole piece is of great interest.

74.   Karl Jung, *Modern Man in Search of a Soul*, Kegan Paul, Trench, Trubner, 1933, pp. 227-228.

75.   The reader may like to refer to Arthur Koestler, op. cit., for many suggestive comments on related topics. Also Ghiselin, op. cit., especially the quotations from Poincaré.

76. *The Mystery of Being*, 2, Chicago, Gateway Editions, 1960, p. 113ff.
77. See note 19, pp. 134-135.
78. Even if they are of *ambiguous* structures.
79. Quoted from *The Dawn of Day*, Preface, in Matson and Montagu, op. cit., p. 344.

Chapter II

1. See the discussion of translation in Lodge, op. cit., pp. 23-26.
2. Edward Sapir, *Language*, Harvest Books, p. 222.
3. Paul Valéry, *Œuvres*, Tome I, Pléiade, 1957, pp. 120-121.
4. C. Day Lewis, *Collected Poems*, Jonathan Cape/Hogarth Press, 1954, p. 299.
5. A similar point is made by Erlich, op. cit. : ' The application of linguistic methods which isolate individual words as semantic centres of attraction is far too mechanical a procedure, as it does not take full account of the poetic context '. Erlich is here outlining the views of Boris Eichenbaum, who objected to the atomistic critical approach of V. Vinogradov in his study of Anna Akhmatova's poetry. See Erlich, op. cit., pp. 233-234. See also J. R. Firth, op. cit., p. 7.
6. The reader may like to attempt translations, into any languages he or she knows, of the texts analysed in this book, and consider how stylistic considerations bear on the process.

Chapter III

1. Quoted by William Empson, op. cit., p. 30.
2. ibid., pp. 31-32.
3. *Articulate Energy*, Harcourt Brace, 1955, pp. 41-42.
4. Compare S. Levin's notion of ' coupling ', *Linguistic Structures*, Mouton, 1962.
5. See also note 1, p. 136.
6. In *Revaluation*, ' Milton's Verse ', Peregrine, 1964.
7. *Paradise Lost*, Book 1, 1.
8. *Revaluation*, pp. 44-45.
9. The symbolism here is as follows :

/ : phrase boundary; // : clause boundary; /// : sentence boundary; ⟪. . .⟫ : interrupting clause; ⟦. . .⟧ : rank-shifted clause*; → : run-on; →» : stronger run-on; ⇒» : strongest run-on.

*Rankshift is a term in Scale and Category grammar indicating a linguistic unit functioning at a lower rank than usual. Here, *how he fell from Heav'n* functions as a nominal group would usually function, e.g. *this*.

The reader may not agree with all points in this analysis. For example, there may be some doubt whether the *grammatical* status of the elements at the end of line 14 and beginning of line 15 is sufficient to ensure that they function *perceptually* as I have assumed. The problem is instructive, being typical of the issues thrown into relief by precise textual work. (See also John Sinclair's comments on the concept of ' arrest ', op. cit. and also ' Lines about " Lines " ', *Current Trends in Stylistics,* Linguistic Research Inc., 1972.)

10.   It is an irony from which no pioneering critic can feel safe that his own programmatic statements can be turned against his inadequate fulfilment of their promise. See Leavis, op. cit., p. 10 : ' In dealing with individual poets the rule of the critic is, or should (I think) be, to work as much as possible in terms of particular analysis – analysis of poems or passages, and to say nothing that cannot be related immediately to judgments about producible texts.'

11.   See W. K. Wimsatt, op. cit. In the chapter on verbal style, Wimsatt states that ' the equalities of meter do not march with but across the parallels of sense '. Sometimes, indeed, this is so but, equally, sometimes not. General principles of this sort inevitably tend to encourage us to overlook the subtly varying relations of formal features to each other. As Osip Brik showed (quoted by Erlich, op. cit., p. 222) such relations tend to be different during different periods. No doubt these variations have more than merely formal significance, as they have within individual poems.

12.   The reader will find *The Muse in Chains,* by E. M. W. Tillyard, Bowes & Bowes, 1958, very instructive on the early development and antipathies of modern critical thinking in Britain.

13.   See note 58, p. 144.

14.   Erlich, summarising Shklovsky, writes that ' juxtaposition on a basis of similarity of two otherwise dissimilar notions is the

omnipresent principle of poetic creation ' (see discussion, op. cit.,
pp. 225-226). Gerard Manley Hopkins defends the same principle
in his ' On the Origin of Beauty ', *The Journals and Papers of
Gerard Manley Hopkins*, ed. Humphrey House, Oxford University Press, 1959, pp. 86-114. S. Levin's notion of ' coupling ' is
not dissimilar.

15.   R. Graves, *Selected Poems*, Penguin, 1961, p. 79.

16.   Freeman anthology, pp. 40-56. (The reader will see for
himself that my use of the term ' dominant ' is not the same as
that of Mukařovský in this paper.)

17.   Freeman anthology, p. 46.

18.   Freeman anthology, p. 44.

19.   Freeman anthology, pp. 43-44.

20.   See a brief discussion of problems connected with foregrounding by Michael Short, ' Some Thoughts on Foregrounding
and Interpretation ', *Language and Style*, vol. vi, no. 2, Spring
1973, pp. 97-108.

21.   The writer has also to ' replace ' features of pitch, loudness,
speed, voice-quality (available to speakers) by other features that
will convey the same information as nearly as possible or provide
the reader with clues which allow him to read adequately.
Donne's use of the line break to suggest intonation and emphasis
in

> I wonder by my troth what thou and I
> Did, till we lov'd . . .

is often cited as an example. Riffaterre, in ' Criteria of Style
Analysis ', has similar points to make.

22.   See Michael Halliday, ' Linguistic Function and Literary
Style ', and discussion (especially comments by Angus McIntosh),
Chatman anthology, pp. 330-368.

23.   This book is not the place for detailed, rigorous exploration
of the possibilities, but the reader will be able to guess at their
intricacy if he or she has done even a little practical work. The
studies which this book contains do not attempt, therefore, to
make explicit the backgrounds relevant to those selected elements
that may be deviant. The reader will realise, however, that these
backgrounds are, in fact, of various kinds, and may find it interesting to attempt to trace their effects as they interact ' behind '
a given work.

24.   In the following study, I have not discussed metrics. Nor,

indeed, many aspects of the poem that are of interest and may well be found to contribute to those overall effects I *do* attempt to describe explicitly. My excuse here, and elsewhere, must be that I am centrally concerned in this book with sketching the outlines of each text, so as to *suggest* how details interrelate within a whole, rather than to discuss all the relevant details themselves. I hope I have taken them into account, however, and that the reader who cares to expand these studies will discover that his findings complement rather than contradict mine. Mine are in the nature of 'caricatures' rather than 'portraits'. (See note 19, pp. 134-135.)

25.   D. H. Lawrence, *Love Poems*, Pocket Poets, Studio Vista, p. 40.

26.   Degas, 'The Tub', 1886, reproduced in *Women Dressing*, Degas, Methuen.

27.   These statements could be made much subtler, of course. *She rises*, in line 1, verse 1, is in a dependent clause, and not at the beginning of the line, and *she stoops* is also in a dependent clause, though at the beginning of a line. It would take a very careful examination to explain why the chain I select here stands out perceptually – if, indeed, readers agree that it does do so. Looking closer, one sees a tendency to vary between the *she* phrases and those which concern other subjects (*the sunbeams, the shadow, her breasts, her shoulders, they, it*): possibly the reader responds to the semantic oscillation, emphasised by line position (the *she* phrases are the only subject-verb groups that come line-initially from line 3 onwards), so that line 6, verse 2, does give the effect of a departure from expectation (see also note 28 below on *sentence*-initial subjects). One also needs to notice the activity and motion of the other subjects, as well as of *she*: with the last sentence, as she and nature merge, a stillness replaces both, through the stillness of a continuing process of concentration. Perhaps the echo of sound as well as sense between *I linger* and *I listen* (*for*) serves to link the two phrases that refer to the observer, and so do draw attention to that aspect of the poem's theme which has to do not with the concentration of the woman's figure itself but with the concentration of attention it evokes in him, to be interpreted no doubt as a representation of Lawrence's view that lovers should be 'single', more intensely 'themselves' rather than mutually 'possessed'. Hence we are reminded of the two poles, *I* and *she*, in both verses (while *I*, as I indicate later, also serves as a device to intensify the impression in verse

2, by allowing for the suggestion that his perception has become so acute that time seems to pass more slowly than normal).

28. See note 27 above. All sentences begin with main clauses, except the first. All sentences that begin with their subject, begin with *she*, except the last. No doubt this contributes to the prominence of the *she* chain of phrases, and consequently to any impression of 'takeover' in line 6, verse 2.

The considerations in this and the previous note serve to show the subtle interaction of features that may condition response.

29. In the context of no rhyme and rhymes like *Watch her, catch her*, I respond to *window, mellow*, as 'full'. Other readers consider *mellow, yellow* the first full rhyme. The point is, of course, that however we describe the rhyme *window, yellow* it is the first that is not due to lexical repetition and therefore strikes the mind as a rhyme rather than the mere repetition of a consonant (or consonant cluster, depending on the phonemic notation) plus *her*. The fuller rhyme *mellow, yellow* serves to relate the shadow to the roses through form as well as semantic suggestion (the 'mellowness' of the shadow relates it visually to the yellow roses, and lays the groundwork for the image that concludes verse 2). (The reader will of course notice the insistence on the sibilants /s/ or /z/ at line-ends, and the frequent appearance of / əʊ / towards the line end: *window, shoulders, mellow, glows as, full-blown, yellow, roses*; *shoulders, golden shadow, glows as, roses*: with the recurrence of *glows as* and *roses* as an off-rhyme more emphatic in verse 2 than in verse 1.)

30. I have already referred the reader to Tynianov's discussion of sequence in verbal art (note 17, p. 133). See also Zefia Lissa, 'The Temporal Nature of a Musical Work', *Journal of Aesthetics and Art Criticism*, 26, 1967-68, 529ff.

31. I use the expression 'key-image' with particular reference to the semantic role the image has in the poem as a whole. Of course, when introduced, it can only strike the reader because it is lexically unusual, and receives the formal emphasis described: subsequent readings, however, must be influenced perceptually, I assume, by the fact that we know that the analogy based on this image is the basis of the analogy between woman and roses, to which each verse builds up, more completely and intensely in verse 2 than in verse 1, culminating in *her golden shadow/Fold on fold, until it glows as/Mellow as the glory roses:*

mellow having been 'transferred' here, from its application to the *shadow* in lines 6-7, verse 1, to a dual application, to *shadow* and *roses*, so acknowledging as it were grammatically the visual feature on which the crucial analogy hinges. (See also note 29 above.)

32. The recurrence of / əʊ /. is represented typographically. Italicised items are recurrent. The lines that link recurrent features serve to indicate the extent to which the two verses trace similar paths through them. *Gloire* and *glory* are bracketed as a cross-language recurrence. *Yellow* and *blown* are, the reader will notice, the only / əʊ / items which do not recur: these are further commented on in the main text.

33. Although *full* can probably be said to be the 'same' lexical item in its two occurrences, *blown* when associated with it loses its original sense almost entirely and can be thought of as merging with *full* in a fixed phrase so that it is only marginally an exception.

34. Again, I am assuming the kind of response to the text which is possibly only after at least one reading (see also note 30 above): the problems raised by repeated receptions of the same text, or piece of music, are of particular interest, since they are unique to sequential arts. We have, in our interpretation of the effect of sequence, to take account both of sequence itself *and* of familiarity. I have tried, informally, to do this, but there is clearly an area here for careful research.

35. D. H. Lawrence, *Selected Literary Criticism*, Mercury, 1964, p. 85. Compare Walter Pater, *The Renaissance*, Mentor, 'Conclusion', pp. 156-159.

36. Text from *The Oxford Book of Ballads*, ed. A. Quiller-Couch, Clarendon Press, 1910. I have taken it that the refrain should appear after each verse, and not only at the beginning and end. This decision bears on the analysis at some points, as will be evident to the reader, but of course many of the features of the described structure remain unaffected if the alternative decision is taken.

37. The use to which demonstratives can be put is of great importance for the writer. See, for example, their role in the opening passages of Wordsworth's *Tintern Abbey*, and Yeats' use of them in *Coole Park and Ballylee* (there is a short discussion of the latter in Chapter 4, pp. 82-84). They are a powerful aid, for instance, in leading the reader to visualise for himself.

38. See the previous discussions of factors bearing upon per-

ceptual prominence, especially Introduction, pp. 17-18 and note 20, and Chapter 1, p. 32 and notes 54-56.

39.   From *The Princess*, section VII, quoted on p. 81, *Tennyson*, selected by W. E. Williams, Penguin, 1953.

40.   Of course, the stability itself cannot be ignored : it plays a traditional lyrical role, serving to highlight auditory features of the poem (such as the phonemic links between *waves, winks, wakens*; *slides, leaves, folds, slips, fold, slip, lost*; or the rhythmical effect of regularity leading up to the pausing of the last two lines). Perhaps it even throws the originality of the poem, once that is understood, into relief. I have not taken space to discuss these relatively minor effects, but they would have to appear in any complete study.

41.   See Allen Rodway, ' By Algebra to Augustanism ', Fowler anthology, pp. 53-67, for a suggestive discussion of some effects of syntactical structure in poetry.

Chapter IV

1.   For many good examples, see David Lodge, op. cit. Mark Schorer has an interesting paper, ' Fiction and the " Analogical Matrix " ', Babb anthology, pp. 338-352, though I am not happy with the priority he gives to metaphor over other aspects of language in his concluding proposals.

2.   See notes 1 and 3, pp. 130-131.

3.   Interesting work has been done on recurrent motifs : in the fairytale by Propp, *Morphology of the Folktale*, Texas, 1968; in the *Decameron*, by Tzvetan Todorov, ' La poétique structurale ', *Qu'est-ce que le structuralisme?*, ed. Ducrot, Paris, 1968. See also R. Barthes and T. Todorov in *Communications*, 8, Seuil, 1966.

The most challenging material is of course that which, while not obviously formulaic, nevertheless appears, impressionistically, to repeat certain structural features. The interesting question may well be not ' What are the similarities?' but, once the formula is grasped ' What are the differences, and how are they related to the individuality, and success or failure, of each story?'

4.   *The Secret Agent*, Dent, 1965, p. 212.

5.   ibid., pp. 262-263.

6.   Ambrose Bierce, *Collected Writings*, The Citadel Press, N.Y., 1963, p. 9ff.

7. *Oliver Twist*, ed., Kathleen Tillotson, Clarendon Press 1966 p. 360. I am indebted to Beatrice Hamer, who drew my attention to this text when we were colleagues at Lancaster University. It is interesting to notice that the text goes on ' At length, when his hands were raw with beating against the heavy door and walls . . .', indicating the effect Dickens expected the passage to produce on the reader.

8. *Collected Poems*, Macmillan, 1958, pp. 275-276.

9. This principle is of fundamental importance not only to literary criticism, but to the teaching of creative writing. In the latter sphere, it is a powerful safeguard against improper interference with the subjects, and appropriate means, of each individual writer.

10. *To The Lighthouse*, Hogarth Press, 1927, ' Time Passes ', p. 201.

11. *The Waves*, Penguin, 1951, p. 128.

12. *Poems and Prose*, Penguin, 1972, p. 27.

13. *Under the Volcano*, Penguin, 1966, p. 18.

14. ibid., p. 212.

15. *The Sound and The Fury*, Penguin, 1972, p. 11.

16. See however the very detailed and worthwhile work done on James Joyce's short story, ' Eveline ', by Seymour Chatman, ' New Ways of Analysing Narrative Structure ', *Language and Style*, vol. II, no. 1, 1969.

17. Though see her fear of contact (p. 118), shown in the insistence on invisibility and the invasive movement and nearness of the animals.

18. She is afraid, but the ' something wild ' that stirs in her heart (p. 118) allies her with the half-wild cat which claws Maurice (p. 127) and which, in the context, appears to indicate Maurice's contact with basic forces of life.

19. She is ' balanced against him ' (p. 119).

20. The more explicitly sexual phrases activating the sexual connotations of words such as *covered* (which appears twice) and investing the notion of touch itself with sexual implications.

21. On p. 128. See also the incident concerning the bowl of flowers on p. 123. Also the occurrence of *closing* in paragraph 1 and of *closed* on p. 123, followed by *closing . . . closing . . . close pressure* on p. 128, all leading up, one might feel, to the ' breaking in ' of Bertie's shell (a phrase which occurs twice, in slightly different forms : see the next sentence, in which each is quoted). (See also *shut*, pp. 121 and 127, for related suggestions.)

22.   On p. 115, Isabel repeatedly represents her feelings as other than they are.

23.   Notice also the rather similar ' picking out ' of an important phrase, by its omission from syntactical patterning, by Conrad (quoted on p. 77 above and discussed pp. 79-81).

24.   Interesting in this connection is the Russian Formalist notion of ' retardation ' (see Erlich, op. cit., p. 245), and also their analyses of character opposition and parallelism in prose (ibid., pp. 243-244).

25.   In a completer study of *The Blind Man* the significance of this episode would have to be fully explored. It seems that his fears are to some degree the converse of theirs, and Lawrence allows the main structural features of the narration to exclude this episode and throw it into relief : had it come, say, while Maurice was in the stables, or even downstairs with his wife and Bertie, the overall pattern of events would have remained simple. It seems right to assume that the episode is thrown into relief by being introduced *outside* this pattern, even though the pattern itself is only visible retrospectively (see note 34, p. 152, for a comparable issue raised by *Gloire de Dijon*).

Chapter v

1.   See general discussion, Introduction, p. 17, and notes 19, 20, 21.

2.   *Collected Poems*, Macmillan, 1958, p. 66, and the variorum edition of Yeats' poems, ed. P. Allt and R. K. Alspach, N.Y., 1957. Not all variants are included.

3.   See comments on figure reproduced on p. 32, and also note 54, pp. 143-144.

4.   See W. Nowottny, op. cit., pp. 39-40 : ' Each aspect of experience has a vocabulary appropriate to it, by use of which we can relate our experience to the mental structure useful for thinking and talking about them. Vocabularies and usages may overlap (the overlap too can be exploited by the poet) but the extent to which usage is discriminated gives the poet ample opportunity to select words and phrases that bring into his poem a particular social and cultural context which will interact with other words and phrases in the poem.' It seems a pity that on the whole this area of poetics has been left so largely to satire – or even to prose.

5.   John Keats, *Poetical Works*, ed. H. W. Garrod, 1958, p. 257.

6.   William Shakespeare, *Hamlet*, ' To be or not to be '.

7.   My discovery of this parallelism owes much to Professor Rutherford of Aberdeen University. He had kindly invited me to speak, from a stylistician's point of view, within the framework of some lectures he was giving on Keats. Following a lecture of his own, he remarked during discussion that Keats' line raised an echo in his mind which he had not yet traced. I was to lecture next day. During the intervening night, I found myself sitting up in bed with the solution presented here. It had come to me in sleep!

Phrases from *Hamlet* frequently come to Keats' pen about the period when the *Ode* was composed. See for instance his reference to *To be or not to be* in a letter to George and Georgiana Keats, dated 14th February – 3rd May, 1819 (the *Ode to a Nightingale* is dated May 1819). *The Letters of John Keats*, ed. M. B. Forman, 1952, pp. 295-341 (esp. p. 306).

8.   Apart from references already given (note 1, p. 130), the reader may like to look through *Literature and Science*, Blackwell, 1955, especially pp. 44-51 and the papers by Guberina, E. R. Vincent, D. I. Masson, A. Closs and Ronald Peacock.

9.   The point is important. The stylistician should, as I see it, avoid narrow assumptions as to what may be relevant (see comments on the narrowness of some *literary* assumptions p. 53). The pressure on a teacher is only too often to provide guidelines which, although they help the beginner to grasp *something* quickly, afterwards obstruct him or her in the development of independent and flexible insight.

10.   See note 5, p. 131, on the grammatical model used here.

11.   Similarly Spencer and Gregory, *An Approach to the Study of Style*, p. 91.

12.   See S. Levin, ' Internal and External Deviation in Poetry ', *Word* (2), pp. 225-237.

13.   Three types of selection are relevant to stylistics : that based on linguistic criteria (a form of applied linguistics), and two types of stylistic analysis, one based on criteria relevant to the exploration of the communicative effectiveness of all texts (involving, for instance, an awareness of the potential effect of deviation and patterning) and the other based on criteria which take account of factors affecting the unique structure of individual texts (such

as the relative prominence of particular features, and the bearing of semantic relevance on their perception). A great deal of research will have to be done before we know just where the boundaries lie between these three kinds of textual study.

14. See Geoffrey Leech's exploration of problems of interpretation raised by a poem of Dylan Thomas: ' " This Bread I Break " – Language and Interpretation ', Freeman anthology, pp. 119-128.

15. The principle that formal emphases, linkages, etc., may be inappropriate or appropriate, but not ' neutral ', should act as a safeguard against descriptive selection embodying evaluation, and then being made to support it (see F. E. Spearshott, op. cit., p. 103). Formal patterning in literature is seen as having *at least to this extent* independence from the level of meaning, even though there may be borderline cases in which formal prominence itself appears to depend on semantic relevance (see pp. 32-33). See, however, S. Levin, ' The Conventions of Poetry ', Chatman anthology, pp. 177-193, where it is argued that the conventions of poetry ' are unique among the elements of poetry in that it is possible to argue that they function exclusively to produce an aesthetic effect '.

16. Again, Spearshott, op. cit., pp. 104-105.

17. See W. Haas, *Essays in Criticism*, 8, 1958; also J. Barzun, ' Misbehavioural Science ', *The Human Dialogue*, ed. Matson and Montagu, pp. 97-108; Angus McIntosh, ' The Problems of Language and Literature ', 9th Annual Conference of University Teachers of English, Wadham College, Oxford, April 4, 1959; and Roman Jakobson, ' Closing Statement: Linguistics and Poetics ', Sebeok anthology, pp. 350-377.

18. See R. Jakobson, *Essais de Linguistique Générale*, Editions du Seuil, 1970, p. 211: ' l'objet de la poètique c'est avant tout de répondre à la question: qu'est-ce qui fait d'un message verbale une oeuvre d'art?' I would doubt that there is any clear dividing line but as we reach more and more towards that end of the spectrum where we feel sure we are dealing with ' art ', we find a fuller and fuller exploitation of the medium. In my view, this means not just the creation of additional patterns, for example, but their use to increase communicative impact. In this view, a relatively ' plain ' text *may* be more truly artistic than a highly ' elaborated ' one, if the structure of the former is relevant to meaning and the structure of the latter irrevelant. But of course not all critics would agree. Clearly, such differences of

opinion must affect not only our critical work but also the way in which we would advise a would-be writer to develop his or her skills.

Selective Index
to the main text

INDEX OF AUTHORS